## History Comes Alive Teaching Unit

# THE AMERICAN REVOLUTION

by Jacqueline B. Glasthal

SCHOLASTIC
PROFESSIONAL BOOKS

NEW YORK • TORONTO • LONDON • AUCKLAND • SYDNEY
MEXICO CITY • NEW DELHI • HONG KONG • BUENOS AIRES

# DEDICATION

To Nick...
and all other rebels
with or without a cause—
past, present, and future.


*"I cannot live without books."*
—Thomas Jefferson


Special thanks to Virginia Dooley for all her patience.
This sure did take longer than I thought it would!

**Mona Mark:** Painting of the Boston Tea Party © 2000
**AP/Wide World Photos:** Portrait of George Washington
**Library of Congress:** Join or Die cartoon (also page 48)

Interior:

**New York Public Library:** 31 [Stokes Collection]
**Scholastic Photo Archive:** 21 (Jean Fritz portrait by Jill Krementz, 1989); 57 (Ann Rinaldi portrait)
**NYPL/Schomburg Center for Research in Black Culture:** 33 (credit, title, letter to publisher from John Wheatley, and
"On being brougnt from Africa to America")
"Spy at Yorktown" © 1981 by Sue Macy. Used by permission of the author.

Scholastic Inc. grants teachers permission to photocopy the reproducible pages from this book for classroom use. No other part of this publication may be reproduced in whole or in part, or stored in a retrieval system, or transmitted in any form or by any means, electronic, mechanical, photocopying, recording, or otherwise, without written permission of the publisher. For information regarding permission, write to Scholastic Inc., 557 Broadway, New York, NY 10012.

Picture research by Dwayne Howard
Cover design by Josué Castilleja
Interior design by Solutions by Design, Inc.
Illustrations by Mona Mark

ISBN: 0-590-31500-5

Copyright © 2003 by Jacqueline B. Glasthal
All rights reserved. Printed in the U.S.A.

2 3 4 5 6 7 8 9 10    40    09 08 07 06 05 04

# CONTENTS

The American Revolution The American Revolution The American Revolution The American Revolution The American Revolution The American Revolution The American Revolution The American Revolution The Ame The American Revolution The American Revolution The American Revolution The American The American Revolution The American Revolution The American Revolution The American

# INTRODUCTION

How do you make a world that no longer exists seem real to students? Clearly, one way is to immerse them in the stories, words, and images of and about that time. And when it comes to the American Revolution, that is exactly what this book will help you to do.

The resources in this guide focus on the period immediately before, during, and after the war. Many activities feature outstanding age-appropriate literature that helps capture the human details as well as paint a broad picture of this period in history. Their purpose is to give students a sense of the people who lived in this era, what their lives were like, and what motivated them—no matter which side they fought for. The reproducible pages in this guide offer students the opportunity to read and analyze primary source accounts from colonial and British perspectives, learn period songs, act out a play about the successful efforts of a spy working for General Lafeyette during the Battle of Yorktown, and much more. Author study pages for Jean Fritz and Ann Rinaldi help students understand more about how historical fiction and nonfiction writers interpret and present the topics they research, and provide ideas for students to read and write about each genre.

One key focus of the activities in this book is to help students identify and understand different perspectives. As students begin to understand that there is always more than one side to every story, they see that not only the colonial soldiers, but the British generals, Hessian mercenaries, Native Americans, slaves of African descent, and women who lived and worked during this period, were also affected—whether they fought in the war or not.

Students should all walk away from this unit of study on the American Revolution with a broader appreciation of the issues involved and the hard choices that people had to make as they decided whether their loyalty lay with the British crown or the "rebels" who had decided to break free of King George's oppressive rule.

# PART 1

# Setting the Scene

> **FOCUS:**
> *What was life like in colonial America, just before the American Revolution?*

## INTRODUCTION

European colonists or their ancestors living in America in the mid-1700s had come to the "New World" for many reasons: religious and political freedom, inexpensive land, and the potential for a better economic future. As long as political leaders back "home" in England allowed them these freedoms, most colonists accepted British rule, and the benefits that went along with it.

There were occasional clashes, however. As early as 1651, for example, a Navigation Act required that wool, sugar, cotton, and tobacco be traded from British ships and only between England and its possessions. The British also imposed "duties," or taxes, on many of these goods. At first the colonists tried to find ways around these laws. Secretly they smuggled goods in from other countries. And, for a long time, the British let the colonists "get away" with this.

# ACTIVITIES

## Life (but not Much Liberty) in the Colonies

 Students build background knowledge about life in the American colonies before the Revolution as they begin a KWL chart, investigate the true meaning of liberty and freedom, and research a historical figure from colonial America.

..................................................

## "Revolutionary" Prior Knowledge

A KWL chart is an excellent way to find out what students already know about a topic, and what questions and misconceptions they still have about it. You may want to do this activity the tried-and-true way, by distributing individual copies of the KWL chart so that students can keep their own records of what they have learned. Alternately, you might use the KWL chart bulletin board display idea below.

### MATERIALS
Tricorn Hat KWL Chart reproducible (page 12)

### WHAT TO DO

🔔 To create a bulletin board display using the Tricorn Hat KWL Chart, enlarge the hat image and post it in the center of the bulletin board. (By pinning index cards with students' comments on the bulletin board, you can reuse the KWL Chart later in your unit.)

🔔 Select an aspect of the war for students to focus on. If you like, use the "Focus" questions that appear at the opening of each chapter in this book for guidance. Post that question at the top of the chart and discuss

as a group what students already know about this topic. Add this information at the top of the chart.

🔔 Encourage students to come up with related questions that they'd still like to have answered. Pin these questions on the left side of the hat. As the class continues through the unit, students should be on the look-out for the answers to their questions. These answers go on the right side of the hat. When the chart is completed, review it as a group so students can see how much they've learned. Invite them to add new questions at the bottom of the chart.

..................................................

## Give Me Liberty — In the Shape of a Poem!

### MATERIALS
Blank sheet of paper

What Liberty Means to Me reproducible (page 13)

### WHAT TO DO

🔔 On a blank sheet of paper, invite students to make up a short list of words and phrases that they associate with the concept of freedom. Their lists might include ways to define freedom (i.e., "doing whatever I want"), privileges that make them feel free (i.e., staying up late), and things that they would do, given the freedom (i.e., "eat as much chocolate as I want, whenever I like").

🔔 After 10 minutes or so, tell students to turn their papers over, and pretend that they are now colonists living in pre-Revolutionary America. In this role, challenge them to make up a new list of words and phrases telling what freedom means to them. When they're done, distribute the What Liberty Means to Me reproducible. Invite students to refer to the two lists they made as they write their poems. Offer students a chance to read their works aloud if they wish. Then post the finished poems on a bulletin board display.

## CLOSE UP: The Liberty Bell

America's famous Liberty Bell was originally ordered in honor of Pennsylvania's 50th birthday as a British colony. It arrived in America from London in 1752. But the very first time it was rung, it cracked! Rather than send it back to England to be recast, the bell was sent to a foundry near Philadelphia. That made it the first large bell ever made in America. The bell was rung to herald many special occasions—including King George III's accession to the throne in 1761. Later it was also used to announce the Declaration of Independence and the British surrender at the end of the war. Unfortunately, the bell cracked again in 1835 and hasn't been rung since.

# In the Backwoods of New York— A Fight for Land

## BACKGROUND

Wars and fighting were not unheard of in the colonies, even before the American Revolution. Ever since 1689, there had been land disputes between French and British colonists, and their respective Native American allies. The culmination of these was the French and Indian War, which took place between 1754 and 1763.

## MATERIALS

*The Matchlock Gun*, by Walter D. Edmonds (Dodd, Mead & Co., 1941)

## WHAT TO DO

🔔 Have students read about the French and Indian War to understand why the relationships between colonists and Native Americans were so tense and often filled with violence. For an historical fiction angle, invite students to read the Newbery Medal-winning picture book, *The Matchlock Gun*. This story offers a view of what life was like for colonists living in the backwoods of colonial New York during the French and Indian War.

🔔 Point out to students that it was this war—fought largely by the colonists themselves—that England later sought to pay for in the form of higher taxes on the colonists. Ask students, *If you were a colonist living at that time, how would this taxation policy have made you feel? Would you have wanted to pay those taxes? Why or why not? What might you have done instead?*

## DID YOU KNOW...?

Many pre-Revolutionary conflicts in the North American colonies had nothing to do with Great Britain or His Royal Highness. For a long time, tensions also ran high between poor tenant farmers and the rich landowners.

# Trading Places

## BACKGROUND

An eighteenth-century colonial main street was lined with stores and craftsmen advertising their wares. Can students envision what such a street might have looked like?

In Newbery Medal-winning *Johnny Tremain*, by Esther Forbes (Houghton Mifflin, 1943), a talented silversmith's apprentice wounds his hand in a furnace accident. Suddenly he needs to find a new trade. While trying to figure out what to do, Johnny wanders the streets of Boston, where shop signs advertise the storekeepers' wares:

> *A pair of scissors for a tailor, a gold lamb for a wool weaver, a basin for a barber, a painted wooden book for a bookbinder, a large swinging compass for an instrument-maker. Although more and more people were learning how to read, the artisans still had signs above their shops, not wishing to lose a possible patron merely because he happened to be illiterate.*
>
> —Chapter III, *Johnny Tremain*

## MATERIALS

**Sign of the Times reproducible (page 14)**

## WHAT TO DO

🔔 Read aloud the selection from *Johnny Tremain* above and ask students to picture the signs Johnny might have passed by.

🔔 Secretly assign each student to one of the eighteenth-century trades listed on the reproducible.

🔔 Have students research what someone with that skill did for a living and then use the Signs of the Times reproducible to create their own shop signs. Be sure that students work with pictures, rather than words, so

that any colonist would be able to clearly understand what service their shop provides.

🔔 When they're done, hang students' signs along the perimeter of the classroom and label each one with a letter.

🔔 Post a list of the trades in the classroom, and challenge students to match each sign with the appropriate trade from the list. If you'd like, have ready a reward for the student who matches the most signs and trades correctly.

🔔 Call on each student to give a detailed oral report on the trade that he or she researched. You might also encourage students to pretend that they worked in that trade, and write up an "Apprentice Wanted" sign to post in their shop window. What skills do they think a young apprentice for this trade might need to have?

# A First Case for Freedom of Speech

## BACKGROUND

In 1735, forty years before the war with England officially started, New York printer Peter Zenger dared to print articles critical of the British-appointed governor of colonial New York. When he was brought to trial, and emerged victorious, it was a huge victory for freedom of the press. That victory would later be remembered, and incorporated into the American Bill of Rights.

## MATERIALS

*The Printer's Apprentice*, by Stephen Krensky (Bantam Doubleday Dell, 1995)

## WHAT TO DO

🔔 Read aloud or have students independently read *The Printer's Apprentice*. In this book, Peter Zenger's case is told through the eyes of a boy in training to become a printer.

After reading the story, organize students into two teams. Tell one that they are on the staff of William Bradford's *New York Gazette*. The others work for Peter Zenger on the *New-York Weekly Journal*. Invite each to put together an issue of their newspaper that might have come out the week of Peter Zenger's trial.

# Remembering "The Good Ol' Days"

## MATERIALS

Colonial People in History Map reproducible (page 15)

## WHAT TO DO

Distribute copies of the Colonial People in History Map reproducible and invite students to select one of the well-known historical figures featured on the page.

Have students research the following about their subject: the colony in which the person grew up, his or her childhood life, occupation, and political or religious beliefs.

Encourage students to think and write about their findings from that subject's perspective. (Of course, lifestyle varied from colony to colony, and also greatly depended on a person's economic status.)

## REVOLUTIONARY RESOURCES

These titles invite students to read about colonial life from a variety of angles.

### FICTION

*Meet Felicity: An American Girl*, by Valerie Tripp, and other Felicity titles in the American Girl series (Pleasant Company Publications, 1991). These titles will give students—particularly girls—a motivating, and non-threatening glimpse at life in colonial Williamsburg, Virginia, just before the outbreak of the war. *Felicity's Cook Book* and *Felicity's Craft Book* contain colonial project ideas, too.

*Night Journeys*, by Avi (Beech Tree, 1979). Feeling that he doesn't belong, Peter York considers running away from his adoptive Quaker family in 1769. Then he finds himself helping out two runaway indentured servants. Here's his opportunity: Will Peter choose to join them when they go?

*Encounter at Easton*, by Avi (Beech Tree, 1980). Part of the same series as the above title.

### NONFICTION

*If You Lived at the Time of the American Revolution*, by Kay Moore (Scholastic, 1998).

*If You Were There in 1776*, by Barbara Brenner (Simon & Schuster, 1994). The author gives readers "a tour" of the times—its cities, farms, ways of worshipping, eating, playing, and surviving—in a tone that makes everyone feel as though they are really there.

### ON THE WEB

The History Place

**http://www.historyplace.com/unitedstates/ revolution/index.html**

Complete time line of the American Revolution with images and links.

### FOR TEACHERS

*Colonial America: Cooperative Learning Activities*, by Mary Strohl and Susan Schneck (Scholastic Professional Books, 1991).

Name_____ Date_____

# Tricorn Hat KWL Chart

FOCUS: _____

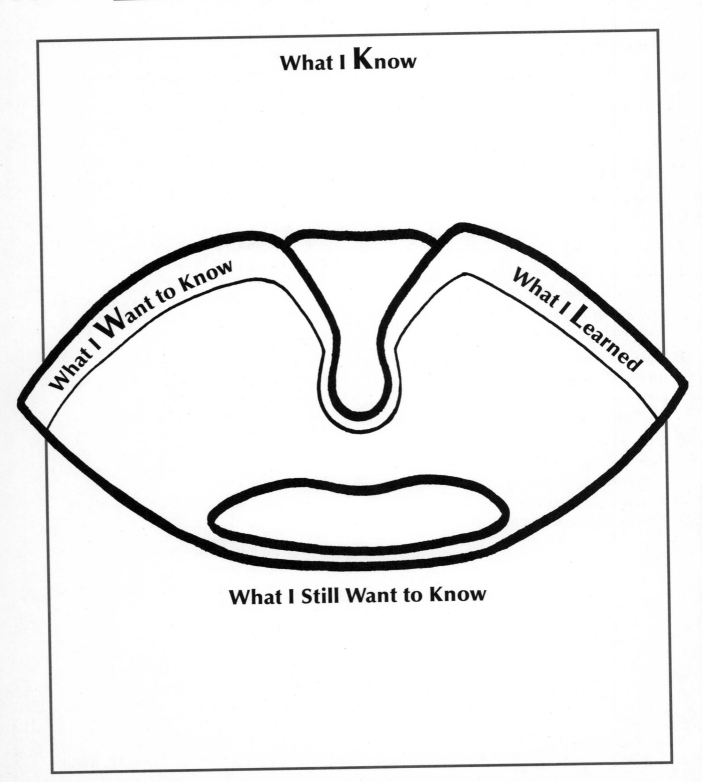

What I **K**now

What I **W**ant to Know

What I **L**earned

**What I Still Want to Know**

# What Liberty Means to Me

What does the word liberty mean to you? Write a poem about it—in the shape of the Liberty Bell! The first line of your poem should start with the letter *L*, the second line with the letter *I*, and so on.

**L** _____

**I** _____

**B** _____

**E** _____

**R** _____

**T** _____

**Y** _____

# Sign of the Times

How might you have earned a living if you lived in colonial times? Pick a trade used in eighteenth-century America. Then create a sign that will make it clear to people what you do. Remember to use pictures instead of words on your sign. After all, not everyone back in those days could read!

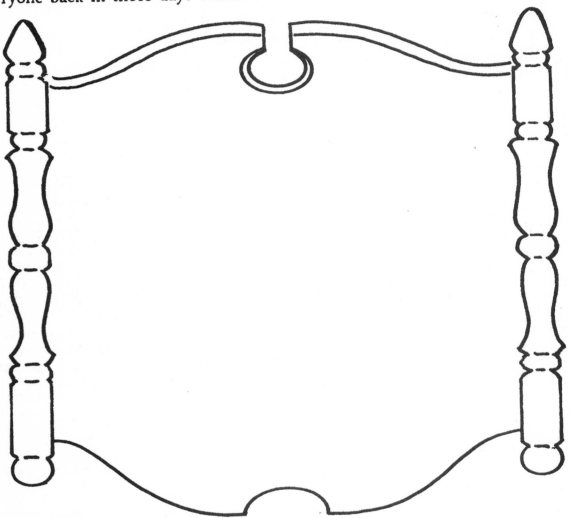

## Eighteenth-Century Trades

| | | | | |
|---|---|---|---|---|
| blacksmith | cooper | gunsmith | printer | tanner |
| bookbinder | cordwainer | hatter | ropemaker | tinsmith |
| butcher | farrier | joiner | shipwright | weaver |
| clockmaker | fuller | miller | silversmith | wheelwright |
| cobbler | glassblower | pewterer | soapmaker | wigmaker |

THINK ABOUT IT: Do people still work in the trade that you selected? If not, why is that? If so, what is it called now, and in what ways has this form of work changed? Would people still recognize a shop specializing in this type of work from the sign that you made?

# Colonial People in History Map

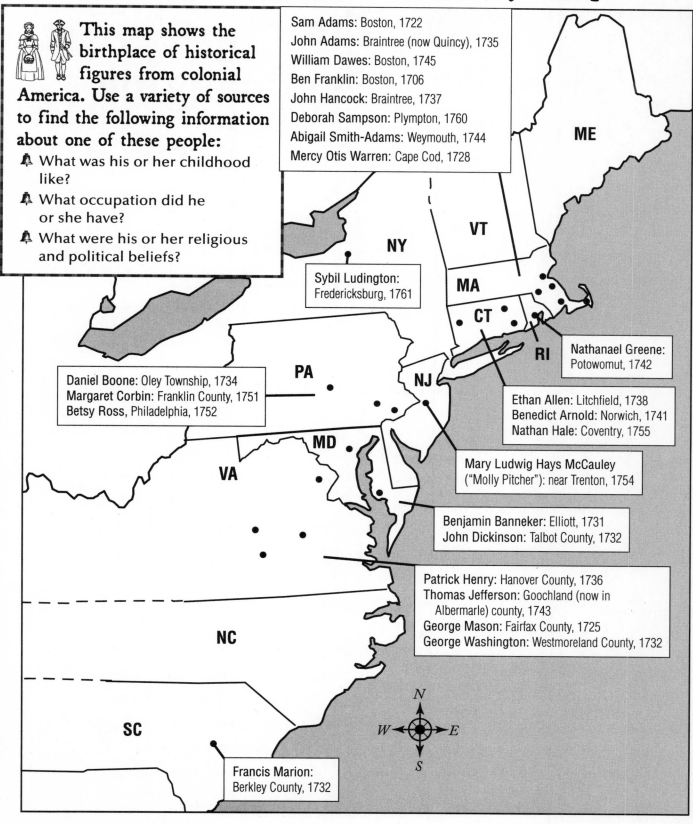

Name_____ Date_____

This map shows the birthplace of historical figures from colonial America. Use a variety of sources to find the following information about one of these people:

🔔 What was his or her childhood like?

🔔 What occupation did he or she have?

🔔 What were his or her religious and political beliefs?

Sam Adams: Boston, 1722
John Adams: Braintree (now Quincy), 1735
William Dawes: Boston, 1745
Ben Franklin: Boston, 1706
John Hancock: Braintree, 1737
Deborah Sampson: Plympton, 1760
Abigail Smith-Adams: Weymouth, 1744
Mercy Otis Warren: Cape Cod, 1728

ME

VT

NY

MA

CT

RI

Sybil Ludington:
Fredericksburg, 1761

Nathanael Greene:
Potowomut, 1742

PA

NJ

Daniel Boone: Oley Township, 1734
Margaret Corbin: Franklin County, 1751
Betsy Ross, Philadelphia, 1752

Ethan Allen: Litchfield, 1738
Benedict Arnold: Norwich, 1741
Nathan Hale: Coventry, 1755

MD

VA

Mary Ludwig Hays McCauley
("Molly Pitcher"): near Trenton, 1754

Benjamin Banneker: Elliott, 1731
John Dickinson: Talbot County, 1732

Patrick Henry: Hanover County, 1736
Thomas Jefferson: Goochland (now in
    Albermarle) county, 1743
George Mason: Fairfax County, 1725
George Washington: Westmoreland County, 1732

NC

SC

N
W ⟷ E
S

Francis Marion:
Berkley County, 1732

# PART 2

# The Times,
# They Were A-Changing

**FOCUS:**

*What changes brought about a rising sense of dissatisfaction from colonists toward British rule?*

## INTRODUCTION

A few years before the French and Indian Wars ended, on March 25, 1760, King George III was crowned King of England. He was 22 years old. Though not everyone in England agreed with them, the new king and his advisors soon made up their minds to tax the American colonists for a large portion of the war debt. The colonists, of course, were miffed. At first they politely debated the issue in pubs and meeting houses throughout the colonies. After all, they were British citizens, too, they reasoned. The king just needed to understand their point of view. But over time, as the colonists started to feel more and more like second-class citizens of the "mother country," their conversations became more and more heated. The question evolved from "What taxes does the crown have a right to impose on us?" to "Why do we even need the crown at all?" The debates grew quite intense at times, as colonists began drawing contradicting conclusions of their own.

# ACTIVITIES

## Loyalist or Rebel?

Students explore the differences between monarchy and democracy, participate in a simulation, read a chronological flow chart, evaluate quotations to determine point of view, debate the merits of taxation, and make predictions with works of historical fiction to better understand the reasons many colonists were dissatisfied with British rule after the French and Indian War.

## Hail to the King!

Help students imagine what it might be like to live in a monarchy instead of a democracy.

### WHAT TO DO

🔔 Have students shut their eyes and pretend that it has just been announced that, due to a new law, the president of the United States will no longer be an elected office. The current president will, like a king, continue to lead the country until the end of his life. At that point, the new law states, the presidency will be passed down to that president's oldest child.

🔔 Ask students to imagine for a moment how this might change the U.S. government we know. What would be different? What kinds of things might stay the same? Would students prefer to have a king rule the land—or do they think electing a president is a better system? Could this kind of change ever really happen in the United States? Why or why not?

🔔 Have students discuss or write a persuasive paragraph or essay supporting their opinion.

## An Overseas Simulation

### BACKGROUND

King George III probably believed that he had the best interests of the colonies in mind when he set his policies. He was also entirely convinced that, because parts of the French and Indian War had been fought on American soil, the colonists should help pay for it. But, some colonists wondered, how could a king in England possibly know what would be best for people thousands of miles away? And, since they were required to pay taxes, shouldn't they have a say in the way they were ruled?

### WHAT TO DO

🔔 Ask students if they think it would be possible to be ruled fairly by a monarchy, "long distance." Why or why not?

🔔 Now, work with another class via the Internet (or, if this is not feasible, with another class in the school or school district) to test the theory. Between the two classes, decide which one will play the part of England and which will be the colonies. Direct the class of rulers "in England" to create a list of rules and regulations that the "colonists" must follow. These rules can—but don't have to—be based on those already used in the "British" classroom. (For example, rules might include specifics on how to behave on the playground, or the proper procedure for passing homework papers to the front of the room.) Once these rules have been established, have the "colonists" discuss them. Are they fair? Do they make sense in the "colonial" classroom? For example, if the "British" class sits in rows and the "colonists" sit at round tables, what happens to the procedure for passing in papers?

🔔 Discuss how the class of colonists should respond to the rules with which they disagree, and how they should react if "England" refuses to change them. If you like, continue the simulation with a series of e-mails (or other types of correspondence) in which players on both "continents" try to resolve their differences. Can students come up with a set of rules that are amenable to both sides?

..................................................

# Let's Role-Play: "Are You Mad Enough Yet for War?"

## MATERIALS

**Liberty Tree Flow Chart reproducible (page 22)**

## WHAT TO DO

🔔 Hang a sign on one wall of your classroom labeled "Loyalists" and one on the opposite wall labeled "Rebels." Then set the scene for this activity by telling students to imagine that they are loyal British subjects living in the American colonies in 1763. The French and Indian War has just ended, which means no more fighting. Since England won the war, it also means the potential for acquiring more land.

🔔 Now invite your class of "British subjects" to come stand under the sign labeled "Loyalists." Have them listen closely as you read, one by one, the events that took place over the next several years, listed on the Liberty Tree Flow Chart. As they listen, students should decide if any of these events—or the accumulation of them—would convince them to switch their allegiance to the Rebel cause. If so, these students should go stand under the "Rebel"

sign that you posted. (Note that, at any time during this role play, students can opt to move back to the Loyalist side.) To test comprehension, randomly call on students to explain why they're on the side they've chosen, and to discuss as a group the ramifications to the colonists of each decision that the British leaders made.

🔔 When a majority of students have become "Rebels," talk about what happened during this activity. Students may find that it became easier to move to the Rebel side once other students had changed their views. Point out that this is very similar to what actually happened over 200 years ago among the colonists, before our nation was born.

🔔 As an alternative, distribute copies of the reproducible and have students complete the activity individually, writing on the back of their papers their explanation for why they would choose one side or the other. Which events would have influenced them the most? You can also use the flow chart as the basis of a bulletin board display.

🔔 After completing the activity, post the following quotation from John Adams on the chalkboard:

> *"The Revolution was in the minds and hearts of the people, and this was effected from 1760 to 1775, in the course of fifteen years, before a drop of blood was shed…"*

Discuss this quotation in relation to the role-playing activity that students just completed. Ask: *In your own words, what does this quotation mean? How are the quotation and the role-playing activity related? Based on the events listed on the flow chart, was there anything England or the colonists could have done to prevent tensions from getting out of hand? If so, what?*

## CHALLENGE

Encourage students to write their own "What if..." stories telling how future events might have changed if King George and the colonists had managed to reach a compromise. They might also wish to role-play a conversation between a representative from the colonies and one from England. What might the two discuss if they both wanted to come to an understanding and avoid a war?

# A Taxing Activity

## BACKGROUND

In many ways, the king's firm stance on taxes actually helped unify the colonists. In colonial days, each colony had its own governing body that acted separately from the others. These colonial governments had little to do with each other—until their fury over taxes united them.

## WHAT TO DO

🔔 Have students discuss why the various taxes imposed by the British so angered the colonists. Then ask students to think about the many different kinds of taxes people pay today. *(There are state and federal income taxes, sales tax, property taxes, and so on.)* Students should understand that these taxes help the government raise money to pay for services, salaries, and overhead. Point out that, because the Continental Congress did not have the power to raise tax dollars, George Washington had a difficult time paying his troops!

🔔 Once students have some idea about the role of tax dollars today, work together to figure out about how much money in sales tax students pay weekly for the items they buy.

🔔 Brainstorm as a class some of the services, local and national, that come out of these tax dollars. *(These services include education, a police force, maintenance of public roads, local*

*representation in national government, and so on.)*

# Parent Problems

## BACKGROUND

Rebel? Loyalist? Which side would your students have taken—and what would they have done if others in their family had decided differently? Can your students imagine disagreeing so strongly with their parents that they'd fight for the other side in a war?

## WHAT TO DO

🔔 Have students try to imagine themselves in this scenario. Then invite them to read independently the first few chapters of one of the books listed below in which the main character grapples with this or a similar dilemma.

🔔 When they reach a crucial deciding point in the story, have students assume the voice of the main character, and write a "Dear Abby"-type letter seeking advice.

🔔 Invite students to "send" their letters to another classmate who has selected a different title. The recipient can then write a response advising the main character about what he or she should do and then share that response with the letter's author. This is a good time to evaluate predictions and discuss the most likely outcomes.

🔔 Finally, students should finish reading their literature selection to find out how the problem was actually resolved.

Titles that work well for this activity include:

*My Brother Sam Is Dead*, by James Lincoln Collier and Christopher Collier (Four Winds Press, 1974). A boy is torn by his father's and brother's opposing political views in the Tory town of Redding, Connecticut.

*Early Thunder,* by Jean Fritz (Puffin, 1987). About a boy who's been raised as a Tory in pre-revolutionary Salem, Massachusetts, and is forced to decide on political views for himself.

*Sarah Bishop,* by Scott O'Dell (Scholastic, 1988). A 15-year-old girl's Tory father is killed by Patriots, and their home burned down.

...........................................................

# Who Said It: Tory or Whig?

## MATERIALS

**Who Said It: Tory or Whig? reproducible (page 23)**

## WHAT TO DO

🔔 Distribute copies of the Who Said It: Tory or Whig? reproducible. Have students complete the sheet on their own, and then go over the answers as a class.

🔔 If there are cases in which students disagree, figure out as a group whether or not it's possible that the answer is not entirely cut-and-dry. For example, though Preacher Cleghorn (in *Sarah Bishop*) believes that everyone should "strive to be understanding of those who have different thoughts," he does not go so far as to say how to deal with irreconcilable differences. Can students still infer from his statement which side he'd probably choose?

*Answers to page 23: 1. T; 2. T; 3. W; 4. T; 5. W; 6. T*

## DID YOU KNOW…?

The Sons of Liberty raised their first Liberty Pole in 1770 in what is now New York City's City Hall Park. In Boston, patriots often met at a stately old elm tree in Hanover Square, known as the Liberty Tree. Liberty Trees and Liberty Poles sprung up throughout the colonies as a place for colonists to meet, protest, give speeches, and hang messages related to their cause. When they could, Loyalists would tear down these symbols—but the rebels would simply put them up again!

## REVOLUTIONARY RESOURCES

**For a very broad overview of the issues and events surrounding the Revolution, invite students to flip through one of these short nonfiction books.**

*In 1776,* by Jean Marzollo (Scholastic, 1994). A very short overview of the war, told in rhyme.

*King George's Head was Made of Lead,* by F.N. Monjo (Coward, McCann & Geoghegan, 1974). A simple, rhythmic retelling of events that occurred at the outbreak of the American Revolution, told from the point of view of a statue of King George III that actually stood in Manhattan's Bowling Green. The statue was later melted down by the colonists for bullets!

*The Liberty Tree: The Beginning of the American Revolution,* by Lucille Recht Penner (Random House, 1998).

# Author Study: Jean Fritz

Perhaps it is because Jean Fritz was born in China, where she attended a British school, that so much of her writing focuses on early American history. "No one is more patriotic," she once wrote, "than the one separated from his or her country. No one is as eager to find roots as the person who has been uprooted."

Primarily through her biographies, Fritz has informed readers all about such "major players" in the American Revolution as Sam Adams, John Hancock, Paul Revere, Patrick Henry, and even King George III! Here are some ideas for using Fritz's books to help students learn more about the War of Independence as they focus on her unique nonfiction writing style.

## Literature Activities With Jean Fritz Books

### Hall of Fame I

Beginning with some of the famous figures that Fritz writes about, have students help you create a "Hall of Fame" bulletin board of famous names and faces from the American Revolution. To do this, have each student draw a picture of a different historical figure and then post, alongside the picture, some fun facts about the person he or she drew.

### Hall of Fame II

Using the information on your "Hall of Fame" bulletin board, invite students to participate in a game of "Who's Who." To start, pin the name of a key Revolutionary figure on the back of each player. (Students should not know whose name is pinned to their own backs!) To learn who they are, students should walk around the room asking other players "yes" or "no" questions. When they think they know their identity, students should return to their seats. Then, go around the room and have students

guess (explaining which clues they used to decide) as you unpin their nametags to see if they were right!

### Most Deserving "Founding Father"

After reading *Why Don't You Get a Horse, Sam Adams?* challenge students to argue that Sam Adams deserves the title "Father of Our Country" even more than George Washington. Or, students might wish to argue that another famous figure (Ben Franklin, Crispus Attucks, Thomas Jefferson, Thomas Paine—or even King George III) deserves the title even more.

## BOOKS BY JEAN FRITZ

### SHORT BIOGRAPHIES

*Can't You Make Them Behave, King George?*

*George Washington's Breakfast*

*Shh! We're Writing the Constitution*

*And Then What Happened, Paul Revere?*

*Where Was Patrick Henry on the 29th of May?*

*Will You Sign Here, John Hancock?*

*What's the Big Idea, Ben Franklin?*

*Why Don't You Get a Horse, Sam Adams?*

### LONGER WORKS

*The Cabin Faced West*

*Early Thunder*

*Homesick: My Own Story*

*Traitor: The Case of Benedict Arnold*

### ON VIDEO

*Six Revolutionary War Heroes*

### ABOUT JEAN FRITZ ON THE WEB

Teacher Vision

http://www.teachervision.com/lessonplans/lesson-10939.html

Transcript of an interview and links to photos of the author.

# Liberty Tree Flow Chart

This flow chart lists some major events that led to the American Revolution. Follow the branches on the tree (starting with circle #1) to decide if you would have joined the rebel troops had you lived in colonial America at that time.

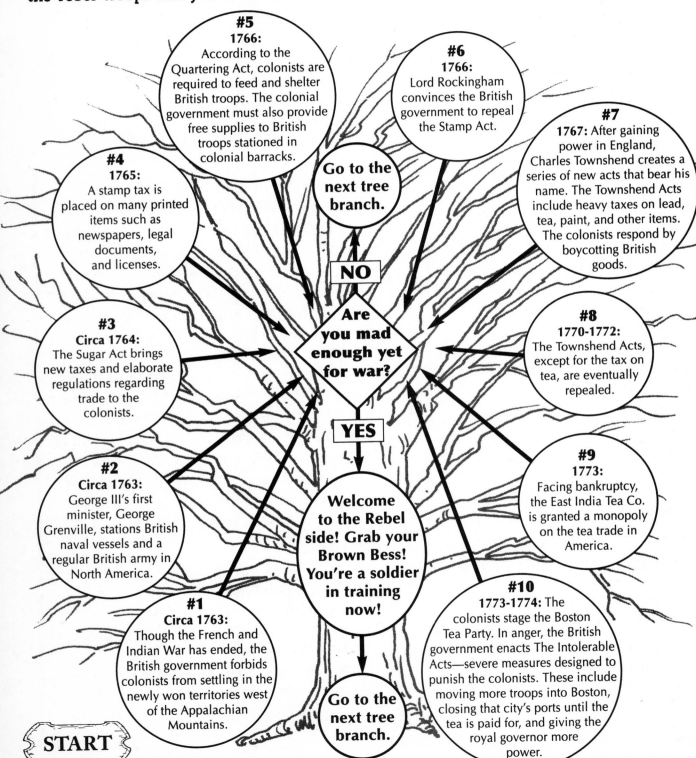

**#5**
**1766:**
According to the Quartering Act, colonists are required to feed and shelter British troops. The colonial government must also provide free supplies to British troops stationed in colonial barracks.

**#6**
**1766:**
Lord Rockingham convinces the British government to repeal the Stamp Act.

**#7**
**1767:** After gaining power in England, Charles Townshend creates a series of new acts that bear his name. The Townshend Acts include heavy taxes on lead, tea, paint, and other items. The colonists respond by boycotting British goods.

**#4**
**1765:**
A stamp tax is placed on many printed items such as newspapers, legal documents, and licenses.

**Go to the next tree branch.**

**NO**

**Are you mad enough yet for war?**

**#8**
**1770-1772:**
The Townshend Acts, except for the tax on tea, are eventually repealed.

**#3**
**Circa 1764:**
The Sugar Act brings new taxes and elaborate regulations regarding trade to the colonists.

**YES**

**#9**
**1773:**
Facing bankruptcy, the East India Tea Co. is granted a monopoly on the tea trade in America.

**#2**
**Circa 1763:**
George III's first minister, George Grenville, stations British naval vessels and a regular British army in North America.

**Welcome to the Rebel side! Grab your Brown Bess! You're a soldier in training now!**

**#1**
**Circa 1763:**
Though the French and Indian War has ended, the British government forbids colonists from settling in the newly won territories west of the Appalachian Mountains.

**#10**
**1773-1774:** The colonists stage the Boston Tea Party. In anger, the British government enacts The Intolerable Acts—severe measures designed to punish the colonists. These include moving more troops into Boston, closing that city's ports until the tea is paid for, and giving the royal governor more power.

**START**

**Go to the next tree branch.**

# Who Said It: Tory 🎩 or Whig 🎩?

As tensions grew between England and the colonists, people found themselves siding with one group or the other. Those willing to go to war to defend their rights were called **Whigs, Patriots**, or **rebels**. Those against open defiance of the king were known as **Tories** or **Loyalists**. In some cases, Whigs and Tories agreed on how England should treat the colonists. They disagreed, however, on what to do when England refused.

DIRECTIONS: Read the following statements made by characters in various works of historical fiction. Write a "W" next to each one that you think was made by a Whig. Write a "T" next to each one that you think was made by a Tory. Then put a checkmark next to the opinions with which you agree.

1. ☐ "God meant man to obey. He meant students to obey their fathers, he meant men to obey their kings…. Do you really think you know better than the King and those learned men in Parliament?"

   —Mr. Meeker in *My Brother Sam Is Dead,* by James Lincoln Collier and Christopher Collier.

2. ☐ "Let us strive to be understanding of those who have different thoughts from ours. For we share a common speech and do worship the same all-merciful God."

   —Preacher Cleghorn in *Sarah Bishop,* by Scott O'Dell

3. ☐ "Papa says the English will make us slaves, just as we were in Germany. This is our land now. We have our own government, our own churches, our own schools. If we want to keep them, we have to fight for them."

   —Jacob Volpert in *An Enemy Among Them,* by Deborah H. DeFord and Harry S. Stout

4. ☐ "There's three thousand miles between us and England…. It makes governing difficult. We can't expect all the privileges of the parent state…. We have to sacrifice. For the present, even our charter itself, if necessary. And whatever it means, acknowledge Parliament freely as our master."

   —Daniel Leonard in *Early Thunder,* by Jean Fritz

5. ☐ "I've come around to putting freedom before the empire…. We have to have meetings. We have to have a say in how our lives are run. We have to talk as long as talking's possible. And if that doesn't work…. If they start to fight, we'll have to fight."

   —Daniel West in *Early Thunder,* by Jean Fritz

6. ☐ "[The people] are asked to choose between, on the one hand, peace and good order under the just and lawful authority of their sovereign, and lawlessness and the arbitrary rulings of self-appointed upstarts on the other."

   —Colonel James Ogilvie in *Rebecca's War,* by Ann Finlayson

# PART 3

# Beginnings in Boston

> **FOCUS:**
> *How and when did open hostilities erupt between the American colonists and the British?*

## INTRODUCTION

For a long time, the colonists tolerated the taxes, trade restrictions, and lack of representation in Parliament. But over time, their complaints turned to more active forms of protest: boycotts, disobedience, and open hostility toward the Crown, the tax collectors, and the customs officers sent to enforce the king's laws. Finally, in the Fall of 1768, British soldiers were sent to America. Prior to this time, British soldiers had been sent to protect colonists from Indian attacks. Now their assignment was to maintain order among the colonists themselves. Not only did colonists resent the Crown treating them like disobedient children, they resented the "lobster backs" who patrolled their communities and hired themselves out for cheap wages in their spare time. On March 5, 1770, tensions came to a head in an incident that came to be known as the "Boston Massacre." From that point on, it seemed, the colonists were clearly headed toward war with the British.

# ACTIVITIES

## A Taxing Situation Fuels Rebellion in the Colonies

Students learn how life changed for the colonists under British occupation. Focusing on the events of the Boston Massacre and the Boston Tea Party, students participate in a trial simulation, evaluate political propaganda, compare the motives behind Loyalist and Rebel actions, and read related primary source documents.

## Troops in Boston

Show students how the British military role changed in the colonies by comparing their initial presence to that of police officers and their later occupation to that of soldiers.

### WHAT TO DO

🔔 On the chalkboard, create a Venn diagram with two overlapping circles. Label one "Police" and the other "Soldiers." Point out that both are hired to maintain order and protect the peace. Write these common traits in the area where the circles overlap.

🔔 Ask students how the roles of police officer and soldier differ. Write their responses in the appropriate spaces of each circle.

🔔 Explain to students that in many ways, the British soldiers who came to the colonies before 1768 were more like police officers than soldiers. Their main purpose was to ensure order and protect the colonists. Those soldiers who came later were sent over to

enforce the king's laws—often against the people's will.

## Soldiers on Trial

### BACKGROUND

As students have probably gathered by now, the American colonists clearly had some legitimate frustrations with their British leaders. At the same time, they didn't always respond in the most honorable ways. While writing articles, boycotting products, holding nonviolent demonstrations, writing resolutions, and petitioning the government qualify as acceptable forms of protest, intimidating, threatening, and physically attacking government officials do not!

Legal-minded patriot John Adams must have agreed. That's why, despite his political beliefs (or maybe because of them!), Adams agreed to defend the British soldiers involved in the Boston Massacre. He felt very strongly that they were as entitled to a fair trial as any colonist.

Using the information on The Boston Massacre: You Be the Jury! reproducible, challenge students to hold their own mock trial for the British soldiers who shot and killed five colonial civilians on March 5, 1770.

### MATERIALS

**The Boston Massacre: You Be the Jury! reproducible (page 30)**

### WHAT TO DO

🔔 Before the trial begins, assign one or more

students to research and play each of these roles:

- John Adams, lawyer for the soldiers (the defense)
- a lawyer for the colonists (the prosecution)
- witness: Private Hugh White
- witness: Edward Garrick
- witness: Captain Preston
- more witnesses: one or more impartial observers who saw what happened

🔔 You—as the judge—should give each lawyer the opportunity to question and then cross-examine all witnesses. Then have the rest of the class act as jurors to reach a verdict: Based on what they've heard, were the soldiers guilty of murder, or were they acting in self-defense? (In actuality, Preston and six other soldiers were acquitted because the jury determined that Preston had never given an order to fire; only two were found guilty on the lesser charge of manslaughter. As punishment, they were branded on the thumb and dismissed from the Army.)

🔔 Conduct a debriefing. Tell students that later in his life, John Adams called his part in this trial "one of the best pieces of services I ever rendered my country." Why do students think he felt that way? Have students research Adams' other accomplishments. Then, based on what they know about him and the trial, see if students agree that this was the best service he ever rendered his country. If so, why? If not, what was?

## Political Propaganda

### MATERIALS

**What's Wrong With This Picture? reproducible (page 31)**

**sheets of drawing paper**

### WHAT TO DO

After completing the mock trial (see Soldiers on Trial activity above) or having students study the Boston Massacre, distribute copies of the What's Wrong With This Picture? reproducible. It shows a copy of Paul Revere's famous engraving, inaccurately depicting the Boston Massacre. Based on what students now know about the

---

### EXTENSION: British Occupation

**Ask students to read one or more of the books that follow, which will help them imagine what it might be like to have soldiers living in their homes, instating curfews, and enforcing other unwelcome laws and restrictions. Students can then explore their ideas by acting out a scene or writing an essay based on one of these stories.**

Titles that work well for this activity include:

*Rebecca's War*, by Ann Finlayson (Frederick Wayne, 1972). The British have taken over Philadelphia, and two officers are assigned to live in Rebecca's home. Can 14-year-old Rebecca keep them from finding the gold ingots and secret documents that the Rebels have asked her to guard?

*The Bells of Freedom*, by Dorothy Gilman Butters (Smith Peters, 1984). Jed Crane, an indentured servant, has been bought by a counterfeiter during the British occupation of Boston. But when his new master is jailed, Jed finds out, for the first time, what freedom really means.

*Hope's Crossing*, by Joan Elizabeth Goodman (Houghton Mifflin, 1998). In the summer of 1777, a band of Long Island Loyalists burn and raid 13-year-old Hope Wakeman's home, in search of her soldier father. When they find he isn't there, they decide to kidnap Hope instead.

event, see how many of the inaccuracies they can find. (*The picture shows the colonists as unarmed, and the soldiers fighting on command, in unison. There are no black Patriots such as Crispus Attucks, in the scene. The scene shows a rifle barrel in a window of "Butcher's Hall." [In none of the testimony was any such rifle mentioned.] And "Butcher's Hall" was actually The Custom House, where Private White was standing guard when the incident began.*)

Challenge students to create their own more accurate illustrations of the so-called Boston Massacre. They can draw one image to counter the Revere image or illustrate the event with a series of drawings by dividing a page in quarters to create four boxes that can serve as frames for four sequential illustrations. Invite students to explain what they drew with picture captions and/or a short oral presentation.

## DID YOU KNOW...?

On March 5, 1770— ironically the very day of the Boston Massacre— Parliament repealed the Townshend Act. They kept the tax on tea in place, however, because King George III firmly believed that "there must always be one tax to keep up the right." Still, most colonists went back to buying British goods—some simply limiting their boycott to tea products. Instead they'd drink coffee smuggled in from the Dutch West Indies, or they'd brew their own tea from flowers, herbs or dried fruit leaves.

# Tea Party Tunes

## BACKGROUND

In 1773, England went one step further with their tea tax—they gave the East India Company a monopoly on tea. This meant that if colonists wanted the beverage, they would *have* to buy it from this company! Even though the

tea would not be that expensive, the decision infuriated colonists. If England could decide who sold tea, they realized, the Mother Country could decide who sold any product! In protest, Sam Adams and other "Sons of Liberty" staged an event that they later named the "Boston Tea Party." On the night of December 16, citizens dressed as Native Americans poured 342 crates of tea leaves from East India Company ships into Boston harbor. A few days later a patriot penned this rallying song in honor of the event:

*Rally, Mohawks! Bring out your axes,*
*And tell King George we'll pay no taxes*
*On his foreign Tea.*

## MATERIALS

Revolutionary Tea reproducible (page 32)

## WHAT TO DO

🔔 Review the events of the Boston Tea Party with students. (You might read aloud the background section above.)

🔔 Invite students to make up additional lyrics to the song, telling about what happened on the night of the Boston Tea Party. (The song in its entirety can be found at **http://www.sit-rep.com/h10F3.htm**.)

🔔 Distribute copies of the Revolutionary Tea reproducible. It contains the lyrics of another song about the Tea Party that became popular in colonial days. As they read it, be sure students understand that "the old lady over the sea" represents England and the disobedient daughter represents the colonies.

🔔 Consider staging a classroom reenactment of the Boston Tea Party, making these tunes a part of the production.

# Phillis Wheatley: Revolutionary Poet

## BACKGROUND

At age 20, Phillis Wheatley (a slave) became the first African American and the second female in America to publish a book. In this activity, students read a poem from Wheatley's book, along with a short history of the poet, written by John Wheatley, her owner, and originally printed as part of that book's preface.

## MATERIALS

About Phillis Wheatley reproducible (page 33)

## WHAT TO DO

🔔 Distribute copies of the About Phillis Wheatley reproducible and have students read the poem and letter independently or as a class.

🔔 Use these questions as discussion starters:

- *Imagine that, like Phillis, you were forced to leave your home and family when you were seven years old. What might your adjustment have been like? How are these hardships like the ones you think Phillis had to overcome? How might they be different?*

- *According to her poem, what did Phillis gain by coming to America? Based on his letter, would John Wheatley have agreed with her assessment? What makes you think so?*

---

## EXTENSION: Celebrate Phillis Wheatley Day!

**In 1985, the governor of Massachusetts declared February 1 to be Phillis Wheatley Day. Here are some additional activities you and students can do to honor Phillis Wheatley on that day—or any time of year:**

**1.** Two of Wheatley's poems about the Revolutionary War—"On the Arrival of the Ships of War, and Landing of the Troops" (about the autumn day in 1768 when the British took over Boston) and "On the Affray in King Street, on the Evening of the 5th of March" (about the Boston Massacre) have been lost except for the titles. After researching these events, and reading more of Wheatley's work, invite students to make up their own poems about the events, emulating her writing style.

**2.** Before a publisher would accept her work, Phillis and her owners were asked to provide proof that she'd written the poems herself. (Since most slaves were illiterate, the publisher was suspicious.) To comply, the Wheatleys arranged for her to go before a committee of prestigious Bostonians, including John Hancock,

Governor Thomas Hutchinson, and Reverend Samuel Cooper. For a fictional version of this interrogation, see chapter 25 of Ann Rinaldi's novel *Hang a Thousand Trees with Ribbons: The Story of Phillis Wheatley*. Read this portion of the book aloud to students. Then ask students what *they* would have asked Phillis, and what they think of the idea of such an interrogation.

### Books About Phillis Wheatley

#### NONFICTION

*The Collected Works of Phillis Wheatley*, edited by John Shields (Oxford University Press, 1989).

*Poems of Phillis Wheatley: A Native African and a Slave* (Applewood Books, 1995).

*Revolutionary Poet: A Story About Phillis Wheatley,* by Maryann N. Weidt (Carolrhoda Books, 1997).

#### FICTION

*Hang a Thousand Trees with Ribbons: The Story of Phillis Wheatley*, by Ann Rinaldi (Harcourt Brace, 1996).

- *Phillis wrote many pro-Revolutionary poems during the War of Independence. Why, as a slave, might she have had such strong feelings about this war?*

- *Based on the first lines of her poem, would you conclude that Phillis considered herself a religious person? What makes you think so? What do these lines say about life in America at that time?*

## DID YOU KNOW...?

Though Phillis Wheatley was a patriot, it was a British publisher who finally agreed to publish her poetry. That's why her most political works, such as "To His Excellency, George Washington," were excluded from the book. Later, Washington wrote to thank her for her kind words in that poem. He also invited her to visit him, which she later did.

## REVOLUTIONARY RESOURCES

### FICTION

*The Boston Coffee Party*, by Doreen Rappaport (HarperCollins, 1988). An easy reader, based on a true occurrence, in which two young sisters help a group of Boston women get coffee from a greedy merchant.

*The Fifth of March*, by Ann Rinaldi (Harcourt Brace, 1993). A fictional account of the Boston Massacre from the point of view of an indentured servant living in John Adams' house.

*The Journal of William Thomas Emerson: A Revolutionary War Patriot*, by Barry Denenberg (Scholastic, 1998). Part of the My Name is America series, this book describes in journal format the escalating hostilities between colonists and the British in the year preceding the war.

### NONFICTION

*The Story of the Boston Tea Party: Cornerstones of Freedom*, by R. Conrad Stein (Children's Press, 1984). A short nonfiction explanation, with some background information, a time line, glossary, and index.

*One More River to Cross: The Stories of Twelve Black Americans* by Jim Haskins (Scholastic, 1992). Includes a short yet detailed account of the Boston Massacre in the chapter on Crispus Attucks.

*Songs and Stories from the American Revolution*, by Jerry Silverman (Millbrook Press, 1994). Includes a map of Revolutionary War battle sites.

### ON THE WEB

Database of the U.S. National Archives & Records Administration
**http://www.archives.gov/research_room/research_topics/revolutionary_war/revolutionary_war_pictures.html**

Find pictures of the Revolutionary War, including a 1774 Paul Revere engraving titled "The Able Doctor, or America Swallowing the Bitter Draught."

A poem, "Crispus Attucks," by Olivia Bush [a.k.a. Olivia Ward Bush-Banks] (1869-1944), can be found in *Original Poems* by Olivia Bush (Louis A. Basinet Press, Providence RI, 1899), or on the Internet at
**http://digital.library.upenn.edu/women/bush/poems/bo-attucks.html**

Name_____ Date _____

# The Boston Massacre: You Be the Jury!

Not all witnesses who testified at the "Boston Massacre" trial agreed on what happened. Based on the testimony given in court, however, the following information is believed to be true.

DIRECTIONS: Using these facts, hold a classroom trial for the soldiers accused of killing Crispus Attucks, Samuel Gray, James Caldwell, Samuel Maverick, and Patrick Carr—all "victims" of the Boston Massacre. Then, as a class of jurors, decide: Based on what you've heard, were the soldiers guilty, or did they simply act in self-defense?

## FACTS OF THE CASE

1. Edward Garrick, a wigmaker's teenage apprentice, instigated [started] the incident by harassing Private Hugh White, a British soldier on duty. This type of hostile behavior toward the king's soldiers had become quite common. The soldiers, on the other hand, were under direct orders not to shoot at anyone, since no war had been declared.

2. Private White hit Garrick with one end of his musket.

3. Garrick ran away, but soon returned with more people. Before long, a crowd of hostile civilians (including Crispus Attucks) had formed. White yelled for military reinforcements. Captain Thomas Preston heard the cry and arrived with seven more soldiers.

4. The civilians taunted the soldiers, pelting them with sticks, stones, and snowballs. One soldier, hit by a flying object, fired his rifle, presumably [supposedly] by accident.

5. Captain Prescott never gave his men any orders to fire. Instead, he shouted out, "Don't fire! Hold your fire!" At the same time, though, people in the crowd called out things like "Come on, you lobster scoundrels—fire if you dare!"

6. Soon many rifles were going off. By the time it was over, five men had been killed and many others were injured.

# What's Wrong With This Picture?

Paul Revere, the famous American patriot and craftsman, made this engraving of the Boston Massacre. But, historians say, there are many inaccuracies in it!

DIRECTIONS: Based on what you know about the incident, can you find five or more things about the picture that are incorrect?* When you're done, draw your own picture, showing how the scene might have really looked.

* See "The Boston Massacre: You Be the Jury!" for a brief outline of the event.

# Revolutionary Tea
## (a traditional song)

There was an old lady lived over the sea

And she was an Island Queen;

Her daughter lived off in a new countrie,

With an ocean of water between.

The old lady's pockets were full of gold.

But never content was she.

So she called on her daughter to pay her a tax

Of three pence a pound on her tea,

Of three pence a pound on her tea.

"Now, Mother, dear Mother," the daughter replied,

"I shant'do the thing you ax;

I'm willing to pay a fair price for the tea.

But never the three penny tax."

"You shall," quoth the mother, and redden'd with rage,

"For you're my own daughter, you see.

And sure, 'tis quite proper the daughter should pay

Her mother a tax on her tea.

Her mother a tax on her tea."

The tea was conveyed to the daughter's door,

All down by the ocean's side;

And the bouncing girl pour'd out ev'ry pound,

In the dark and boiling tide.

And then she called out to the Island Queen,

"Oh, Mother, dear Mother," quoth she,

"Your tea you may have when 'tis steep'd enough,

But never a tax from me,

But never a tax from me."

# About Phillis Wheatley

Phillis Wheatley was the first African American and the second female in America to publish a book. Read these pages from her book of poems, written just before the Revolutionary War. As you read John Wheatley's letter to the publisher and Phillis Wheatley's "On Being Brought from Africa to America," consider Wheatley's perspective as a literate slave and how she might feel about the colonists' fight for independence from Britain.

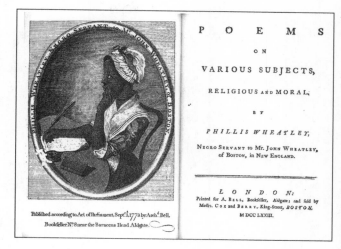

The following is a Copy of a LETTER sent by the Author's Master to the Publisher.

PHILLIS was brought from *Africa* to *America*, in the Year 1761, between Seven and Eight Years of Age. Without any Assistance from School Education, and by only what she was taught in the Family, she, in sixteen Months Time from her Arrival, attained the English Language, to which she was an utter Stranger before, to such a Degree, as to read any, the most difficult Parts of the Sacred Writings, to the great Astonishment of all who heard her.

As to her WRITING, her own Curiosity led her to it; and this she learnt in so short a Time, that in the Year 1765, she wrote a Letter to the Rev. Mr. Occom, the *Indian* Minister, while in *England*.

She has a great Inclination to learn the Latin Tongue, and has made some Progress in it. This Relation is given by her Master who bought her, and with whom she now lives.

JOHN WHEATLEY.

*Boston, Nov. 14, 1772.*

## POEMS

### On being brought from A F R I C A to A M E R I C A.

'TWAS mercy brought me from my *Pagan* land,
Taught my benighted soul to understand
That there's a God, that there's a *Saviour* too:
Once I redemption neither sought nor knew.
Some view our sable race with scornful eye,
" Their colour is a diabolic die."
Remember, *Christians*, *Negros*, black as *Cain*,
May be refin'd, and join th' angelic train.

# PART 4

# This Is War!

**FOCUS:**
*How did a few violent outbreaks
turn into a war?*

## INTRODUCTION

Many colonists disapproved of the tea dumping and may have even been willing to pay for it—except that they frowned on England's reaction even more! Six months after Paul Revere rode down to New York and Philadelphia to tell of the Boston Tea Party, he was back on the road again announcing that, as punishment, the British had closed Boston Harbor. Immediately people in other colonies began sending food and supplies to keep the citizens of Boston from starving. Then the Patriots learned that the British were readying themselves for a secret mission to Lexington, where rebel leaders Sam Adams and John Hancock were staying, and Concord, where the Patriots had a weapons arsenal. Quickly Revere was summoned and told to prepare for his next journey. It would turn out to be his most famous ride of all.

# ACTIVITIES

## A Revolution Begins...

Students study Paul Revere's famous ride and the Battles of Lexington and Concord, focusing on the various perspectives of those involved.

## Paul Revere's Famous Ride

### MATERIALS

"Paul Revere's Ride" by Henry Wadsworth Longfellow, available at a number of Web sites, including the University of Toronto's site: www.library.utoronto.ca/utel/rp/poems/longfe30.html

### WHAT TO DO

🔔 As a class, read aloud Longfellow's famous 1860 poem, "Paul Revere's Ride."

🔔 Challenge students to research the factual inaccuracies it contains (the list below highlights the most blatant). If you feel that this activity is too challenging for your students, or too time-consuming, share the following inaccuracies with students, and have them identify the places in the poem where these statements are made.

- *Revere was not "on the opposite side" when the signal lights were lit in the old North Church tower that night; he was actually the one who directed others to light it. That way his friends in Charlestown would know to have a horse waiting for him.*

- *Revere was not the only Patriot rider that night, as the poem implies; many others also helped spread word of the British plans.*

- *Before he had completed his ride, Revere was captured and his horse confiscated. He never made it to Concord that night. (Samuel Prescott was the only Patriot messenger who did.)*

🔔 Once students have identified these inaccuracies in the poem, challenge them to rewrite it so that all the information in it is true.

## Pick a Viewpoint

### BACKGROUND

A rich selection of age-appropriate literature written about the American Revolution offers students an opportunity to discuss different viewpoints on Paul Revere's famous ride.

### MATERIALS

What's in a Name? reproducible (page 38)
*Back to Paul Revere!*, by Beatrice Gormley (Scholastic, 1994) (optional)
*Mr. Revere and I*, by Robert Lawson (Little, Brown, 1953) (optional)
*The Secret of Sarah Revere*, by Ann Rinaldi (Harcourt Brace, 1995) (optional)

### WHAT TO DO

🔔 Point out to students that when friends disagree, it tends to be because they each have a different viewpoint about something. To make the point, suggest an incident that everyone in your classroom has witnessed—such as an argument on the playground. Select a few students to describe what they saw. Where their perspectives differ, discuss why this might be. Was it because they were standing at different angles? Because they come from different backgrounds? Did it have to do with the role each student played?

🔔 (Optional) Introduce students to one or more of the literature selections and ask them to figure out the perspective from which each one is told.

🔔 Distribute copies of the What's in a Name? reproducible and have students read the humorous poem that gives an account of the famous night from the viewpoint of one of Revere's lesser-known compatriots.

🔔 Discuss the point of view used in this account of that famous night. Then have students brainstorm other people, animals, or inanimate objects that might have viewed the event differently. (For example, how might a British soldier's horse have seen the event?) Each student can then tell the tale—either in writing or in an oral presentation—from one of these points of view. When they're done, have students compare and discuss these imagined perspectives.

# Many Sides to Every Story: The Battles of Lexington and Concord

## BACKGROUND

When the battles of Lexington and Concord were fought, the colonists had yet to start an army, or appoint George Washington its leader. Most colonists who fought that day were members of local militias who had heard what was going on through a complex domino-like communication system, set off when Paul Revere and William Dawes left Boston. But what actually happened at Lexington and Concord on April 19, 1775, who fired the first shot, how organized the rebels were, and whether one side—the rebels or redcoats—acted more cruelly than the other, may never be known. Whatever the details, though, most historians agree on the outcome: These events were the official start to the American Revolution.

## MATERIALS

**The British Perspective reproducible (page 39)**

*Sam the Minuteman* and *George the Drummer Boy* by Nathaniel Benchley (HarperCollins, 1987)

## WHAT TO DO

🔔 As a class, read Nathaniel Benchley's two easy readers, *Sam the Minuteman* and *George the Drummer Boy*, which tell about the battles at Lexington and Concord from a Colonist and British point of view respectively.

🔔 Distribute copies of The British Perspective reproducible and assign students to read, individually or in pairs, Lord Percy's report to General Gage.

🔔 Drawing on the Benchley stories and Lord Percy's report, prompt students to think about how a colonist's version of the battle events might have differed from Lord Percy's. What details did he omit that a rebel would have included?

🔔 After a little more research, have students work independently or in pairs to write one or more of the following fictional journal entries about what transpired that day:

**1.** The events of that day from the point of view of a British soldier on his way to Lexington in the wee hours of that morning.

**2.** That same soldier's thoughts later that day, on the way back to Boston.

**3.** The thoughts of a minuteman standing out on the Lexington green just before the redcoats arrive.

**4.** That same soldier's thoughts later in the afternoon, fighting from behind a stone wall as the British march back toward Boston.

🔔 Invite students to share their writings with the class.

# Remembering Lexington and Concord

## BACKGROUND

On July 4, 1837—62 years after the battles of Lexington and Concord—Ralph Waldo Emerson's "Concord Hymn" was first read at the Old North Bridge in Concord, Massachusetts. That's where "the shot heard 'round the world" was fired, when rebels first killed a British soldier. The skirmish had begun six miles away, in Lexington, a few hours before.

## MATERIALS

"Concord Hymn" reproducible (page 40)

## WHAT TO DO

🔔 Review what happened at the Battles of Lexington and Concord (see the previous activity, Many Sides to Every Story: The Battles of Lexington and Concord, and the literature suggestions in the Revolutionary Resources section).

🔔 Distribute copies of the "Concord Hymn" reproducible and have students read Emerson's famous poem.

🔔 Ask students to imagine that they are former minutemen listening to the 1837 reading. In their younger days they had taken part in the battles that this ceremony commemorates. How do they feel about the ceremony? What memories does it bring back for them? In a letter or speech, have students imagine what they would want to tell the crowd about what had occurred that day.

## DID YOU KNOW...?

It was next to impossible to take careful aim with a colonial musket. Shooters had to turn their heads away so as not to be blinded by the flashback from their own guns! Because of this, experts estimate that, at the battles of Lexington and Concord, only one out of every 300 or so rebel bullets successfully found their mark!

## REVOLUTIONARY RESOURCES

### FICTION

*April Morning*, by Howard Fast (Bantam Books, 1961). More advanced readers will enjoy this excellent fictionalized account of the first hours of the war, told from a 15-year-old's point of view, as he is forced into manhood.

### NONFICTION

*Lexington and Concord: Cornerstones of Freedom*, by Deborah Kent (Children's Press, 1998).

*Paul Revere: Cornerstones of Freedom*, by Gail Sakurai (Children's Press, 1997).

*Which Way to the Revolution?: A Book About Maps*, by Bob Barner (Holiday House, 1998). Cute little mice describe the route Paul Revere took on his famous ride.

# What's in a Name?

## by Helen F. More

I am a wandering, bitter shade;
Never of me was a hero made;
Poets have never sung my praise,
Nobody crowned my brow with bays;
And if you ask me the fatal cause,
I answer only, "My name was Dawes."

'Tis all very well for the children to hear
Of the midnight ride of Paul Revere;
But why should my name be quite forgot,
Who rode as boldly and well, God wot?
Why should I ask? The reason is clear—
My name was Dawes and his Revere.

When the lights from the old North Church
    flashed out,
Paul Revere was waiting about,
But I was already on my way.
The shadows of night fell cold and gray
As I rode, with never a break or pause;
But what was the use, when my name was
    Dawes?

History rings with his silvery name;
Closed to me are the portals of fame.
Had he been Dawes and I Revere,
No one had heard of him, I fear.
No one has heard of me because
He was Revere and I was Dawes.

# The British Perspective: An Account of Lexington & Concord

## as told by Brigadier-General Hugh Percy to General Thomas Gage

In obedience to your Excellency's orders I marched yesterday morning at 9 o'clock with the 1st brigade and 2 field pieces, in order to cover the retreat of the grenadiers and light infantry in their return from their expedition to Concord. As all the houses were shut up, and there was not the appearance of a single inhabitant, I could get no intelligence concerning them till I had passed Menotomy, when I was informed that the rebels had attacked his Majesty's troops who were retiring, overpowered by numbers, greatly exhausted and fatigued, and having [expended] almost all their ammunition—and at about 2 o'clock I met them retiring through the town of Lexington—I immediately ordered the 2 field pieces to fire at the rebels, and drew up the brigade on a height.

The shot from the cannon had the desired effect, and stopped the rebels for a little time, who immediately dispersed, and endeavoured to surround us, being very numerous. As it began now to grow pretty late and we had 15 miles to retire, and only 36 rounds, I ordered the grenadiers and light infantry to move off first; and covered them with my brigade sending out very strong flanking parties which were absolutely very necessary, as there was not a stone wall, or house, though before in appearance evacuated, from whence the rebels did not fire upon us. As soon as they saw us begin to retire, they pressed very much upon our rear guard, which for that reason, I relieved every now and then.

In this manner we retired for 15 miles under incessant fire all round us, till we arrived at Charlestown, between 7 and 8 in the evening and having expended almost all our ammunition. We had the misfortune of losing a good many men in the retreat, though nothing like the number which from many circumstances I have reason to believe were killed of the rebels. His Majesty's troops during the whole of the affair behaved with their usual intrepidity and spirit nor were they a little exasperated at the cruelty and barbarity of the rebels, who scalped and cut off the ears of some of the wounded men who fell into their hands.*

* Note: In actuality, the British lost more men than the rebels during their march back to Boston. And, as far as historians know, no cruelty or barbarity as that described above occurred.

History Comes Alive Teaching Unit: The American Revolution  Scholastic Professional Books

# Concord Hymn

## by Ralph Waldo Emerson

By the rude bridge that arched the flood,
Their flag to April's breeze unfurled,
Here once the embattled farmers stood,
And fired the shot heard 'round the world.

The foe long since in silence slept;
Alike the conqueror silent sleeps;
And Time the ruined bridge has swept
Down the dark stream which seaward creeps.

On this green bank, by this soft stream,
We set today a votive stone;
That memory may their deed redeem,
When, like our sires, our sons are gone.

Spirit, that made those heroes dare
To die, and leave their children free,
Bid Time and Nature gently spare
The shaft we raised to them and thee.

# PART 5

# War of the Words: The Mighty, Mighty Pen

**FOCUS:**

*How did the "Founding Fathers"
help start a new nation?
What role did their words—and the
words of others—play in this war
and in history?*

## INTRODUCTION

There's an old expression that goes "actions speak louder than words." But when it comes to the American Revolution, words spoke volumes also! In a way, it was a "war of the words"; words preceded, instigated, and followed many major events of the war. The war began with words in the form of enactments by the British telling the colonists what they could and couldn't do. The flames of resistance were fanned by the words of staunch rebels like Patrick Henry, Sam Adams, and Thomas Paine. And the Revolution was sealed with the famous written words of Thomas Jefferson and his collaborators in the Declaration of Independence. In this section, students take a look at some of the words, expressions, speeches, and literature that played a big part in the war.

# ACTIVITIES

# The Language of the War

Students identify famous words written by leading figures of the Revolution and use selections from their writings and speeches to explore and debate the meaning behind the words. Students also play word games with terms and expressions used in colonial times to build vocabulary while learning about history through language.

## Fighting Words!

### BACKGROUND

In January of 1776, in a pamphlet called *Common Sense*, Thomas Paine urged colonists to declare their independence from England. Within three months, over 120,000 copies were sold. Before long about one out of every 20 colonists owned one! Clearly this document had a major influence on people at that time. *Common Sense* was not the only document that played a major part in the war effort, however, and students will become familiar with a few other important documents in this activity.

### MATERIALS

Fighting Words! reproducible (page 46)

### WHAT TO DO

🔔 Distribute copies of the Fighting Words! reproducible and have students identify the famous statements.

🔔 Challenge students to select one or more of the documents to research. They can investigate the purpose and sentiment behind each one.

🔔 If you have access to the animated School House Rock! video, *History Rock*, use this to inspire students to write their explanations in musical form!

*Answers to page 46: 1. c; 2. e; 3. a; 4. d; 5.b*

### DID YOU KNOW...?

Mary Katherine Goddard was owner and postmistress of the only print shop in Baltimore, Maryland, in 1777 when she got an important order—to print the first official version of the Declaration of Independence! After doing so, Goddard paid post riders to deliver it throughout the colonies.

## Vocabulary Building, Colonial-Style

### BACKGROUND

Though many believe otherwise, it is unlikely that during his famous ride of 1775 Paul Revere ever shouted those famous words, "The British are coming!" He may have called out "The king's army is coming!" Or possibly, "The regulars!" "The redcoats!" "The lobster backs!" "His Lord's ministerial troops!" or even "The king's men!"—but not "The British!" After all, though they disagreed with England on many issues, most colonists at that time still thought of *themselves* as British subjects!

### WHAT TO DO

🔔 Review colonial-era synonyms for "the British" using examples in the background section above.

🔔 Ask students to think of other terms they know that had synonyms in colonial times.

Generate a list of at least 25 words. To help students get started, post one of the two words in each pair that follows in a column on your chalkboard: lobster back/redcoat; Tory/Loyalist; patriot/rebel; sentry/guard; and militia/army. See if students can give you the synonym.

🔔 Let each student create his or her own Colonial Bingo game board writing one word in each box until the card is full of words from the list. Words should be written in random order so that each card is different.

🔔 While students create their cards, write down each word on the list on a slip of paper, and place all the slips of paper in a hat or bag.

🔔 To play Colonial Bingo, randomly pick out these words, calling them one by one. Have students cover the *synonym* for each word called on his or her Bingo game board. (For example, if you call out the word *patriot*, students can cover up the word *rebel*—but not the word *patriot*.) The first student to correctly cover all the words in a row, column, or diagonal wins.

🔔 Play the game as many times as you like to help students improve their vocabulary, or laminate the cards and place them in a classroom activity center so students can play on their own. The word strips can also be used to play "Colonial Concentration," a game in which students lay out the cards, blank-side-up, then try to turn over the matching synonym pairs.

**Colonial Words Bingo**

| Lobster back | sentry | Great Britain | minuteman | book binder |
| Patriot | munitions | Tory | courier | guard |
| soldier | Whig | Free Space | England | Brown Bess |
| weapons | musket | militia | Loyalist | Redcoat |
| messenger | army | publisher | Rebel | cobbler |

## EXTENSION: Name That Word/Word That Name!

Occasionally, a person's deeds can help to create a new word or phrase in the English language. Two examples from the American Revolution stand out. A "Benedict Arnold" is synonymous with *traitor*. And a person's "John Hancock" is his or her signature.

After sharing these two examples with students, post some other famous names from the American Revolution on the chalkboard: George Washington, Thomas Jefferson, Paul Revere, Betsy Ross, and Phillis Wheatley, for example. Have students create their own definitions for these names (and use it in a sentence!), based on what each of these famous Americans represents.

# Pardon the Expression

## BACKGROUND

Like synonyms, learning the derivation of an expression can go a long way toward improving a student's vocabulary and knowledge base. In some cases it can also show the connection between language and history! This activity invites students to work with idiomatic expressions that originated in colonial times.

## MATERIALS

**Express Yourself! reproducible (page 47)**

## WHAT TO DO

🔔 Distribute the Express Yourself! reproducible and instruct students to work on it independently or in small groups. If students have never heard an expression before, or are not sure what one means, encourage them to use the information provided to take a stab at figuring it out.

🔔 Review the reproducible as a class.

🔔 When students understand the expressions, challenge them to use each one in a sentence with an appropriate contemporary meaning.

🔔 Share—and compare—the new sentences students have written as a class.

*Answers to page 47: **a.** an object with all its parts; **b.** quarreling or involved in a confrontation or disagreement; **c.** unexpected good fortune—usually money; **d.** agree to try something, not knowing for sure what they'll get; **e.** get together to have a good time; **f.** sleep soundly; **g.** cheap or thrifty*

# Poor Richard's Rattlesnake

## BACKGROUND

Ben Franklin was a man of many talents. He was an inventor, scientist, diplomat, printer, writer…and occasionally even a cartoonist! According to some historians, his famous rattlesnake cartoon (see page 48), which was first used in 1754 to convince colonists to band together against attacking Native Americans, was the first political cartoon ever published on American soil. Later the cartoon was used in the patriot cause as well.

## MATERIALS

**From the Pen of Ben Franklin reproducible (page 48)**

## WHAT TO DO

🔔 Enlarge and make a transparency of the rattlesnake cartoon on the reproducible.

🔔 Project an image of the cartoon for the class to see and guide students to read the cartoon.

🔔 Invite students to do some research on rattlesnakes that might help explain why they were used to represent the thirteen colonies. Here are some explanations, and

comparisons, that were given at the time:

- *Rattlesnakes are indigenous to no other part of the world.*
- *They don't have eyelids—so, like Americans, they are vigilant.*
- *Rattlesnakes never begin an attack, nor surrender—so they must be noble, forgiving, and brave.*
- *Rattlesnakes never do harm without warning—so they are generous.*
- *When they are undisturbed and in peace, rattlesnakes hide their weapons.*
- *Rattlesnakes are stronger than they look.*
- *Rattlesnakes prefer to stay alone, and only turn to others when they need to for survival.*
- *Rattlesnakes are beautiful in youth, and their beauty increases with age.*

🔔 Once students understand these comparisons made between rattlesnakes and Americans, invite them to suggest other creatures that could represent the United States, either today or during the Revolution. Be sure students can support their suggestions with similar rationale.

# More Ben Franklin Animal Analogies

## BACKGROUND

In addition to his rattlesnake cartoon, the From the Pen of Ben Franklin reproducible contains a short fable penned by Ben Franklin in Revolutionary days. This activity helps students determine the message behind the fable.

## MATERIALS

**From the Pen of Ben Franklin reproducible (page 48)**

## WHAT TO DO

- Distribute copies of the From the Pen of Ben Franklin reproducible.

- Have students read The Whelp and the Mastiff and ask them how the fable relates to the forming of the new nation. In what ways is its message similar to that of the cartoon? In what ways do the two differ?

- After discussing these questions, challenge students to think of a moment from the Revolutionary era that they would like to turn into a humorous cartoon or a fable that conveys a moral message. (You might want to recommend that students use *Stan Mack's Real Life American Revolution* [Avon Books, 1994] for inspiration. This book tells the history of the American Revolution entirely through cartoons.)

- Compile students' cartoons and fables into a book. Challenge students to help organize the contents in chronological order.

## REVOLUTIONARY RESOURCES

### FICTION

*Annie Henry and the Secret Mission*, by Susan Olasky (Crossway Books, 1995). A fictionalized account of Patrick Henry's life from his 10-year-old daughter's point of view.

*Citizen Tom Paine*, by Howard Fast (Grove Press, 1983). Advanced readers may enjoy this fictionalized account of Thomas Paine's life.

### NONFICTION

*Abigail Adams: Witness to a Revolution*, by Natalie S. Bober (Aladdin, 1995). This Boston Globe-Horn Book Award-winning biography uses many of Abigail Adams' own words to retell her life story.

*The American Revolutionaries: A History in Their Own Words*, 1750-1800 by Milton Meltzer (HarperTrophy,1993).

*Common Sense*, by Thomas Paine (Penguin Books, 1986). The original text of this historic pamphlet first printed in 1776.

*Our Country's Founders: A Book of Advice for Young People*, edited by William J. Bennett (Simon & Schuster, 1998)

*Words That Built a Nation*, by Marilyn Miller (Scholastic, 1999).

### VIDEO

*1776* (Columbia Pictures, 1972). Rent and show this film in segments or in its entirety.

### ON THE WEB

History Place

**http://www.historyplace.com/unitedstates/ revolution/decindep.htm**

Audio, copy, and images related to the signing of the Declaration of Independence.

# Fighting Words!

Give credit where credit is due! See if you can match each famous statement below with the speech or document that it comes from. Then, on a separate sheet of paper, explain in your own words what these statements mean, and how each one came to be.

1. _____ "Is life so dear, or peace so sweet, as to be purchased at the price of chains and slavery? Forbid it, Almighty God! I know not what course others may take; but as for me, give me liberty or give me death!"

2. _____ "[B]e it declared…That the said colonies and plantations in America have been, are, and of right ought to be, subordinate unto, and dependent upon the imperial crown and parliament of Great Britain."

3. _____ "Everything that is right or natural pleads for separation. The blood of the slain, the weeping voice of nature cries, 'TIS TIME TO PART…"

4. _____ "We hold these truths to be self-evident:—That all men are created equal; that they are endowed by their Creator with certain unalienable rights; that among these are life, liberty, and the pursuit of happiness…"

5. _____ "I long to hear that you have declared an independency—and by the way in the new Code of Laws which I supposed it will be necessary for you to make I desire you would Remember the Ladies…Do not put such unlimited power into the hands of the Husbands."

## Choices Box

**a.** Thomas Paine's *Common Sense*, published January 9, 1776

**b.** Letter from Abigail Adams to her husband, John, March 31, 1776

**c.** Patrick Henry's speech to the Virginia Convention, March 23, 1775

**d.** *The Unanimous Declaration of the Thirteen United States of America* (The Declaration of Independence), approved by Congress on July 4, 1776

**e.** England's Declaratory Act of March 18, 1766

# Express Yourself!

In colonial America, the expression "Mind your p's and q's" was something a colonial innkeeper might have said to someone who was drinking too much and becoming rowdy. (The p's and q's referred to pints and quarts of drink!) Today the phrase is still used to tell people to mind their manners and behave.

DIRECTIONS: Each expression below also had its origins in colonial times. Read how each one came about. Then write in what you think it means today. When you're done, use each expression in an original sentence on the back of this page.

a. **lock, stock, and barrel:** A colonial musket was usually constructed and paid for in three separate parts—the lock (firing mechanism), stock (wood), and barrel (metal tube). Once completed, the item as a whole was given to its owner, "lock, stock, and barrel." Today this phrase means…

_____

b. **At loggerheads:** A loggerhead was a long metal bar with a ball on one end, used in taverns to heat up beverages. Unfortunately, patrons would also sometimes use them as weapons during a fight. Today when people are "at loggerheads," they are… _____

_____

c. **A windfall:** In colonial days, people were thrilled when strong winds pulled down tree branches, or even whole trees. These "windfalls" made it easier for people to gather their firewood! Today a windfall is… _____

_____

d. **pot luck:** Many meals in colonial days were prepared in a big pot with a mix of ingredients. As it was impolite to ask

what was in these stews, people would have to take "pot luck" when had to dinner at a neighbor's house. Today when people take potluck, they…

_____

e. **a field day:** Citizens would gather annually on muster day to watch the militia drill. This would be a social gathering with food, drink, and conversation. Today when people have a "field day," they… _____

_____

f. **sleep tight:** There were no metal springs in colonial beds. Some, though, did have rope supports between the wooden sides of the bed frame. These could be tightened to insure a good night's sleep. Today, when we say "sleep tight," we mean… _____

_____

g. **skin flint:** a thrifty colonist who needed but was unwilling to pay for a new flint, might take a knife and chip or skin pieces from the old flint until it was serviceable. Today, a person who is described as "a skinflint" is… _____

_____

# From the Pen of Ben Franklin
## "Join or Die": A Political Cartoon

In your own words, what is Ben Franklin trying to say in this cartoon?

_____

_____

_____

_____

_____

## The Whelp* and the Mastiff**:
## A Ben Franklin Fable

A lion's whelp was put on board a ship bound to America.... It was tame and harmless as a kitten, and therefore not confined but allowed to walk around the ship.

A stately...mastiff, belonging to the Captain, despising the weakness of the young lion, frequently took its food by force and beat the whelp up. The young lion nevertheless grew daily in size and strength, and the voyage being long, he became at last a more equal match for the mastiff, who continued his insults and eventually received a stunning blow from the lion's paw.

In the end the mastiff regretted that he had not rather secured the lion's friendship than provoked its enmity.

* A whelp is an animal's offspring    ** A mastiff is a large, powerful short-haired dog

In your own words, what is the moral of this fable?

_____

_____

In what way do the message of the fable and the cartoon relate to one another?

_____

_____

_____

# PART 6

# A Soldier's Story

**FOCUS:**
*What were some of the major battles and highlights of the war? What would it have been like to play a part in the fighting?*

## INTRODUCTION

On the night of June 16, 1776—about 24 hours after the second Continental Congress had appointed George Washington its commander in chief, yet before he could reach Boston—colonists secretly took over Breed's Hill, near Boston. When they were discovered, at the break of dawn on June 17, the British attacked. Eventually, the British emerged victorious, after the American militia ran out of bullets and gunpowder, but not before the rebels had managed to harm or kill over 1,000 of the enemy—more than double the number that their own militia lost.

This was just the first of many battles that were to take place over the next few years as America's fighting forces were transformed into an army. Most had no regular uniforms, and at first they had more allegiance to their colony than their country. But in time this, too, would change.

The next year, in fact, the colonists lost a number of battles, but won critical victories, such as the Battle of Saratoga, that would work to undermine the British hold on America.

# ACTIVITIES

# Redcoat versus Rebel: From Uniform to Battle

Students compare American and British soldiers by reading related literature and completing a story web, plot the movement of Washington's troops on a map, evaluate truths and legends about Washington, and discover the contributions that colonists made to the Revolution, both on the battle field and off—as spies.

## Minutemen Turned Soldiers: Making a Fashion Statement!

### BACKGROUND

Although some militia units of the American Revolution did manage to pull together a distinct uniform, most soldiers left home wearing whatever was available. In *A Young Patriot: The American Revolution as Experienced by One Boy* (Clarion, 1996), Jim Murphy tells the true story of Joseph Plumb Martin, a young New England farm boy who became a soldier: *"Most likely he wore the loose-fitting pants and shirt he wore when hunting, and a pair of well-worn boots. In addition, he brought his own musket, powder horn, cartridge box, tinderbox with flint, a wooden water barrel, and a knapsack with a change of clothes."*

### WHAT TO DO

🔔 Have students use this description and whatever other reference materials are available to draw a picture showing how Joseph may have looked, labeling each item that he carried or wore (musket, tricorn hat, powder horn, and so forth).

🔔 In a separate illustration, have them compare this "uniform" with that of a British redcoat.

🔔 As a class discuss the benefits and drawbacks of the military power and presence of each side. (*The British had more state-of-the-art weaponry at their disposal. However, their artillery was heavier, and their red uniforms made them an easy target for the colonists.*)

🔔 Ask students: *If you could have designed the uniforms, how would you have recommended that each side dress? Keeping in mind that soldiers sometimes marched ten or more miles a day, how many changes of clothes, and other things, would it have made sense for them to bring?*

### CLOSE UP: Time to Muster!

As head of the Continental Army, one of George Washington's first tasks was to transform his units of enlisted men into soldiers. To do this, they needed discipline—and to improve their fighting ability. To that end, soldiers would spend countless hours drilling, marching, and pretend-shooting (so they wouldn't use up precious bullets!) over and over again.

One of the most common firearms used in those days was a musket known as a "Brown Bess." These guns were anywhere from 5 to 7 feet long, and weighed between 10 and 40 pounds. To load this gun, which was sometimes taller than the person carrying it, a soldier had to get out his gun powder, push the powder and a bullet down the gun barrel using a ramrod, and then position the gun on his shoulder before firing. Those who were good at it could let fly three or four bullets a minute. (Once, Ben Franklin even suggested supplying the fighters with bows and arrows instead of guns, as they could shoot four arrows as fast as one bullet!)

## DID YOU KNOW...?

Because money was scarce, the Continental Army couldn't afford uniforms for everyone. Different units often dressed in unique styles, depending on where they were from. As this made it difficult to identify an officer's rank, General Washington eventually established a color coded system in which commanders in chief wore light blue ribbons, major generals wore purple, and so on.

# Mapping the War

## BACKGROUND

Thanks to the resourcefulness of Ethan Allen's Green Mountain Boys, a still-loyal Benedict Arnold, and 25-year-old artillery officer (and former bookseller!) Henry Knox, the British troops were forced to abandon Boston in March of 1776. While they set off for Nova Scotia to reinforce their troops and rethink their strategy, Washington led his men to New York, where he correctly guessed the British would strike next.

But Washington's first battles as leader of the troops, did not go well. The Battle of Long Island was the largest of the war, with the British sending a force of 32,000—including 8,000 hired German soldiers, known as Hessians—to fight Washington's 18,000. More people fought in this battle than probably resided in all of Philadelphia at the time! Luckily, many of Washington's badly outnumbered troops were able to escape, ensuring that they would be back to fight again.

## MATERIALS

Thirteen Colonies Map reproducible (page 58)

*Samuel's Choice* by Richard Berleth (Scholastic, 1990)

Pushpins or circle stickers (a dozen each of two different colors)

## WHAT TO DO

🔔 Read aloud Richard Berleth's excellent picture book, *Samuel's Choice,* to help students envision how Washington's forces struggled through the Battle of Long Island.

🔔 Enlarge to poster-size the Thirteen Colonies Map reproducible by projecting a transparency onto a large sheet of paper and outlining the map image.

🔔 To help students visualize the troops' movements from this point on, post the oversized map of the colonies on a bulletin board. Use two different colored pushpins or circle stickers (e.g., red for the British, and blue for the Patriots) to track the movements of both sides, as the British forced the Americans up to Harlem Heights, White Plains, Fort Washington, then into New Jersey, and finally Pennsylvania.

🔔 Students can take turns moving the pushpins or stickers around as you review the troops' movements as a class.

# Hessians: Not Such Bad Guys After All?

## BACKGROUND

The 29,000-plus German soldiers, known as Hessians, who were hired to fight on the side of the British, were told terrible lies about the colonists. But most of them had been forced to come and didn't truly support the British cause. So, when they found out that the Americans were not horrible ogres, many chose to desert. By the end of the war, close to half of these hired mercenaries had decided to stay on American soil!

## MATERIALS

One title from annotated book list (see end of activity)

Walk in Their Shoes reproducible (page 59)

## WHAT TO DO

🔔 Read aloud one of the books from the list below.

🔔 Invite students to imagine that they are a key Hessian character described in that selection. They have been paid to come here, and they speak English haltingly at best. How do they perceive the people and their surroundings? If given the choice, would they continue to fight for the British, join the American troops, or simply escape into the countryside? If students had found themselves in this situation, what would they have chosen to do?

🔔 Students can create their own story webs to organize their thinking. The web should include a small circle in the center of the page and six larger circles radiating from it. Have students write in the name of the historical fiction character they want to focus on in the center and use the space in the outer circles to describe what the character sensed (heard, saw, felt, smelled), how the character acted (what she or he did), and what the character said.

🔔 Titles that would work well for this activity include:

*Distant Thunder*, by Ruth Nulton Moore (Herald, 1991). Kate and her cousin rescue an escaped Hessian and nurse him back to health.

*An Enemy Among Them*, by Deborah H. DeFord and Harry S. Stout (Houghton Mifflin, 1987). A young Hessian soldier questions his loyalty to his king after spending time as a prisoner on the farm of a German American family in Pennsylvania.

*The Hessian's Secret Diary*, by Lisa Banim (Silver Moon Press, 1996). A colonial girl finds a Hessian soldier's sketchbook during the Battle of Long Island. Is he a spy—or just a runaway soldier who likes to draw?

---

### DID YOU KNOW...?

Unlike the cherry tree tale, General Washington's crossing of the Delaware on Christmas Eve 1776 was not apocryphal. Though he most likely did not stand during the crossing (as he does in Emanuel Leutze's famous painting), the event was so impressive, it convinced many soldiers to extend their stay in the army at least a few weeks.

# Legendary George Washington

## BACKGROUND

By now, most students have probably heard the apocryphal story of George Washington and the cherry tree. According to legend, at the risk of getting in trouble, young George admitted that he had chopped down the prized tree. "Father, I cannot tell a lie," he supposedly said.

This charming but spurious story was invented by the biographer Mason Locke Weems, who wanted to establish the "father of our country" as a good role model. But why make up stories when the truth will do? For example, knowing how little money was available during the American Revolution, Washington refused a salary; at Valley Forge, he wouldn't move into comfortable quarters until huts had been built to house all of his men; and, at the height of his popularity, he turned down a proposal that he be made king—an offer that others might have found too tempting to reject.

## WHAT TO DO

🔔 Using these, and other examples, challenge students to create their own "true life legends" about George Washington's good character and high ideals. If appropriate, have students share their writings with students in younger grades.

## EXTENSION: Cherry Tree Tales

The tale of the cherry tree is not the only made-up story about the "father of our country." After they have read more about Washington, challenge students to put together a list of true facts and exaggerated tales. They may want to use the following resources:

### FICTION

*George Washington's Breakfast*, by Jean Fritz (Putnam & Grosset, 1969). True facts come to light as a boy tries to find out what his namesake used to have for breakfast.

### NONFICTION

*George Washington: The Man Who Would Not Be King* by Stephen Krensky (Scholastic, 1991)

*I Did It with My Hatchet: A Story of George Washington*, by Robert Quackenbush (Pippin, 1989). Explores the myths and realities of Washington's life.

*...If You Grew Up with George Washington*, by Ruth Belov Gross (Scholastic, 1982)

## A Present for the Troops

### BACKGROUND

The historical novel *The Winter of Red Snow: The Revolutionary War Diary of Abigail Jane Stewart*, by Kristiana Gregory (Scholastic, 1996), takes place during the winter that Washington and his men camped out at Valley Forge. In it, Abigail describes a "bounty coat" that her sister is working on. It's a coat with her name sewn inside that she will give to a needy soldier. "Many girls have become brides this way," Abigail explains.

Whether they were looking for a husband or not, it was quite common during the American Revolution for young women to sew clothes for the soldiers. Often they would even sew messages of hope and comfort within the cloth.

## WHAT TO DO

🔔 Read aloud the quotations in the Read-Aloud History box below.

🔔 Invite students to select a soldier (real or fictional) from one of the books that they have read about the American Revolution.

🔔 Ask students: *If you were going to make your character a present to help him or her through the war, what would it be? What message would you attach to the gift?*

🔔 Invite students to draw pictures of their message-inscribed gifts to post around the room.

## READ-ALOUD HISTORY: Sacrifices...

*"Tea I have not drunk since last Christmas, nor bought a new cap and gown since your defeat at Lexington; and what I never did before, have learned to knit...I know this, that as free I can die but once; but as a slave I shall not be worthy of life. I have the pleasure to assure you that these are the sentiments of all my sister Americans."*

—Mercy Warren in a letter to a British soldier

## And More Sacrifices...

*"The situation of the camp [at Valley Forge] is such that in all human probability the army must soon dissolve. Many of the troops are destitute...The horses are dying for want of forage. The country in the vicinity of the camp is exhausted. What consequences have we rationally to expect? Our desertions are...great. The love of freedom, which once animated the breasts of those born in the country, is controlled by hunger, the keenest of necessities."*

—American General James Mitchell Varnum

# A Code for the Turncoats: What Might Their Messages Have Said?

## BACKGROUND

Many colonial spies played a part in conveying critical information from the British to the rebel side. The reading selections below feature codes that may have been used during the war to pass secrets along.

## MATERIALS
(optional reading)

*Emma's Journal: The Story of a Colonial Girl*, by Marisa Moss (Harcourt Brace & Co., 1999)

*The Journal of William Thomas Emerson: A Revolutionary War Patriot*, by Barry Denenberg (Scholastic, 1998)

*U.S. Students' History: Book of the American Revolution*, by Howard Egger-Bovet and Marlene Smith-Baranzini (Little, Brown, 1994)

## WHAT TO DO

- Read aloud related passages from one of the books above or simply discuss the role codes played in helping spies communicate important information safely.

- Help students look up or make up their own spy codes (for example, they might pair each letter of the alphabet to the numbers 1–26 to create a code they can write in numbers).

- Have students select one of the spy names listed in the Investigate a Spy extension activity, or one from a book they're reading, and imagine what secret message one of these spies may have been delivering. Alternately, they can select another event in the war's history and imagine what secrets might have been put into messages at those times.

- With the secret code they have selected or created, students can encode a message that might have been sent by that spy, or during that event.

- When they're done, have students trade papers and try to decipher their partner's messages. Make a game out of having students try to figure out during which battle or event their partner's message was from.

TIP: To make this activity even more fun, have students write their secret messages in invisible ink, using lemon juice. (The messages can then be read by holding them over a light bulb.) Students may be surprised to learn that colonial rebels were the first ever to use invisible ink in an official way!

## EXTENSION: Investigate a Spy

Have students research the names of Revolutionary War spies on either side. (These names include Nathan Hale, Lydia Darragh, and Emily Geiger for the Patriots; and Benedict Arnold, Rebecca Shoemaker, Ann Bates, John Andre, and Lorenda Holmeson for the British.) Students should consider what made these spies act the way they did. Then, using this information, invite students to write a defense of their actions from their point of view.

# This is Your Life, Molly Pitcher!

## BACKGROUND

As some students are aware, women were not only involved in undercover work and assistance on the home front during the Revolution; many were out there in the trenches, too. Some (like Molly Pitcher) became heroines while traveling at their husband's side in the militia. Others (like Tempe Wicke and Sybil Ludington) unintentionally found themselves in a position to play a crucial role in the war. And a few (like Deborah Samson) actually snuck into the army dressed as men!

## MATERIALS

**Molly Pitcher reproducible (page 59)**

## WHAT TO DO

🔔 Distribute copies of the Molly Pitcher reproducible and read aloud the poem with the class.

🔔 Invite students to select Molly Pitcher or one of the other heroines of the war, and research more about her accomplishments.

🔔 To show their research, have students create a "resume" giving highlights of that person's life. They might organize it under traditional categories, including Education, Job History, Skills, and Special Interests.

🔔 Titles that provide background for this activity include:

*I'm Deborah Sampson: A Soldier in the War of the Revolution,* by Patricia Clapp (Lothrop, Lee & Sheppard, 1977). A first-person fictional account based on the true-life story of one of the war's most famous female fighters.

*A Ride Into Morning: The Story of Tempe Wick,* by Ann Rinaldi (Harcourt Brace, 1991). An elaborate story based on the popular myth about Tempe Wick.

*Danbury's Burning! The Story of Sybil Ludington's Ride,* by Anne Grant (Hill & Wang, 1976).

*Those Remarkable Women of the American Revolution,* by Karen Zeinert (Millbrook Press, 1996). Examines the contributions of Patriot and Loyalist women in various arenas—at home, in politics, in the army, etc.

*Scholastic Encyclopedia of Women in the United States,* by Sheila Keenan (Scholastic, 1996). Organized alphabetically by era.

## CLOSE UP: A Look at the War on the Water

In Revolutionary days, shipbuilding was one of the largest industries in Newport, Rhode Island. So it's no surprise that in February, 1776, the first American naval ships sailed from there. Throughout the war, though, America's naval fighting force remained small. Instead, Congress hired privateers—privately owned pirate ships equipped with cannons—to fight, and loot British boats.

Financially, privateers did much better than regular soldiers. Congress felt they had no choice but to let these men keep the spoils of war. (Sailors in the Continental Navy, in comparison, were only allowed to keep half of whatever they managed to take from enemy ships. And soldiers did even worse!)

# REVOLUTIONARY RESOURCES

## FICTION

*Buttons for General Washington*, by Peter and Connie Roop (Carolrhoda Books, 1986.) An easy reader based on the true story of the Darraghs, a Quaker family living in British-controlled Philadelphia in the fall of 1777, who became spies for the rebels, hiding secret messages in the buttons of their 14-year-old son's coat to sneak into Washington's camp.

*Johnny Tremain*, by Esther Forbes (Houghton Mifflin, 1943). A perceptive boy in Boston with a maimed hand finds out that, despite his disability, he can play an important part in the war.

*Phoebe the Spy*, by Judith Berry Griffin (Scholastic, 1977), is based on the true story of Phoebe Fraunces, the daughter of the proprietor of Fraunces Tavern, who disguised herself as a housekeeper to help save George Washington's life.

*The Rifle,* by Gary Paulsen. (Bantam Doubleday Dell, 1997). A subtle case for gun control is made as readers follow the history of a single rifle from its creation in 1768 through its use in the Revolutionary War, and finally into the hands of a modern-day American.

*George Washington's Socks*, by Elvira Woodruff (Scholastic, 1991). Time travelers take part in the crossing of the Delaware.

*Traitor: The Case of Benedict Arnold*, by Jean Fritz (Putnam Books, 1981).

## NONFICTION

*Crossing the Delaware: A History in Many Voices*, by Louise Peacock (Atheneum, 1998). A medley of art, fiction, and actual letter and diary entries convey the authentic feeling of this history-making night.

*A Young Patriot: The American Revolution as Experienced by One Boy*, by Jim Murphy (Clarion, 1996), based on the memoirs of Joseph Plumb Martin, a young soldier enlisted in the Continental Army from 1776 until hostilities ended in 1783.

*In the Line of Fire: Eight Women War Spies*, by George Sullivan (Scholastic, 1996). Contains an account of how Lydia Darragh risked her life to warn General Washington of an imminent surprise attack by the British.

*Paper Soldiers of the American Revolution*, by Marko Zlatich (Bellerophon Books, 1974).

*A Coloring Book of the American Revolution*, by Harry Knill (Bellerophon Books, 1987).

*Underwater Dig: The Excavation of a Revolutionary War Privateer*, by Barbara Ford and David C. Switzer (William Morrow, 1982) This book walks readers through the real-life excavation of the Defense, a shipwrecked privateer discovered in 1972 in Penobscot Bay, Maine.

*Uniforms of the American Revolution Coloring Book*, by Peter F. Copeland (Dover, 1974)

*A Soldier's Life: A Visual History of Soldiers Through the Ages*, by Andrew Robertshaw (Heinemann, 1997).

*The American Revolution: A Picture Sourcebook*, by John Grafton (Dover, 1975).

## ON THE WEB

Spies of the American Revolution

**www.si.umich.edu/spies/index.html**

Primary source documents, images, and short biographies of Revolutionary War spies.

## VIDEO

*The Crossing* (A&E,1999). This fact-based drama with Jeff Daniels tells the story of George Washington leading his troops across the Delaware on Christmas night 1776 to attack the Hessians.

## FOR TEACHERS

*Famous Americans: George Washington and Abraham Lincoln*, by Maria Fleming (Scholastic Professional Books, 1996).

# Author Study: Ann Rinaldi

Ann Rinaldi knew for a long time that she wanted to be a writer. But it wasn't until her son Ron became involved in Revolutionary War reenactments that she decided to try her hand at historical fiction. And, since so many people told her that her first novel about the American Revolution, *Time Enough for Drums,* would never be published, she made up her mind to prove them wrong! As a rebel in her own right (she became an author despite her father's objections), the topic made sense to her. "I went against the grain of what everybody told me," she once said.

Rinaldi is a prolific writer with about 20 titles to her name—eight of them are about the American Revolution, and just about all involve history in some way.

Unlike Jean Fritz, Rinaldi's work is fictional. But like Fritz, she often bases her books on real people and events. Because of this, you might encourage students to compare her fictional works with nonfiction writing about the same topics, keeping in mind these questions as they read: *How does Rinaldi incorporate facts into her fiction? Where and how does she choose to "elaborate" and add fictional elements to her stories?*

## Literature Activities With Ann Rinaldi Books

### Focus on Author Notes

Rinaldi often uses author notes in the back of her books to distinguish facts from fiction. She also tries to relate the incidents or time periods that she's writing about to things that are more relevant and current for her readers. For example, at the end of *The Fifth of March,* Rinaldi compares the Boston Massacre with the 1950s sit-ins over segregation; the 1960s protests over the Vietnam War; and the 1992 Los Angeles Riots. After reading her author's

note, ask students to select and research one of these events and then write a short essay in which they determine whether or not they agree with the comparison.

### Keep Track!

Ann Rinaldi's books alone offer students the chance to virtually "read their way" through the American Revolution. Using the Read Your Way Through the War reproducible (page 60), students can keep track of the books they've read about the American Revolution—both by Rinaldi, and by others.

## BOOKS BY ANN RINALDI

### ABOUT THE AMERICAN REVOLUTION...

*Cast Two Shadows: The American Revolution in the South*

*The Fifth of March: A Story of the Boston Massacre*

*Finishing Becca: A Story About Peggy Shippen and Benedict Arnold*

*Hang a Thousand Trees with Ribbons: The Story of Phillis Wheatley*

*Or Give Me Death*

*A Ride into Morning: The Story of Tempe Wick*

*The Secret of Sarah Revere*

*Taking Liberty: The Story of Oney Judge, George Washington's Runaway Slave*

*Time Enough for Drums*

*Wolf by the Ears*

### ABOUT ANN RINALDI ON THE WEB

Rutger's Ann Rinaldi page

**scils.rutgers.edu/~kvander/rinaldi.html**

Biography, interview link, and bibliography available.

# Thirteen Colonies Map

Follow the movements of Washington's troops during
the Revolutionary War. Mark each battle site with a
star and label that place and date of the battle.

Lake Michigan

Lake Huron

Lake Ontario

Lake Erie

Ohio River

Mississippi River

N
W   E
S

# Molly Pitcher
## by Kate Brownlee Sherwood

'Twas hurry and scurry at Monmouth town,
    For Lee was beating a wild retreat;
The British were riding the Yankees down,
    And panic was pressing on flying feet.

Galloping down like a hurricane
    Washington rode with his sword swung high,
Mighty as he of the Trojan plain
    Fired by a courage from the sky.

"Halt, and stand to your guns!" he cried.
    And a bombardier made swift reply.
Wheeling his cannon into the tide,
    He fell 'neath the shot of a foeman nigh.

Molly Pitcher sprang to his side,
    Fired as she saw her husband do.
Telling the king in his stubborn pride
    Women like men to their homes are true.

Washington rode from the bloody fray
    Up to the gun that a woman manned.
"Molly Pitcher, you saved the day,"
    He said, as he gave her a hero's hand.

He named her sergeant with manly praise,
    While her war-brown face was wet with tears—
A woman has ever a woman's ways,
    And the army was wild with cheers.

Name_____ Date_____

# Read Your Way Through the War

Many books have been written about the American Revolution. And it's no wonder! The war lasted seven long years (or even longer, if you include some of the events leading up to it). How many of these "big moments" have you read about in a book or poem? Use this sheet to keep track. Across from each event, list the related books and their authors. (If you've read so many that you need more space, just continue on the back!)

| Revolutionary War Topic | What Did You Read? |
|---|---|
| The Boston Massacre | |
| The Boston Tea Party | |
| Paul Revere's Ride | |
| The Battles at Lexington and Concord | |
| The Constitutional Conventions | |
| Other famous battles of the Revolutionary War: | |
| Other important events or people of the Revolutionary War: | |

# PART 7

# The World Turned Upside Down

**FOCUS:**
*How did the war end?*

## INTRODUCTION

During the first years of the American Revolution, most fighting between the British and Americans took place in New York and New England. By 1779, though, the action had shifted to the South where British general Cornwallis won several battles in South Carolina and Georgia. In 1781, he decided to try and take Virginia, too. Ironically, despite the Patriots' inferior naval power, it was, in part, military tactics at sea by their new French allies that helped the Americans attain their final victory at Yorktown. While Washington, Lafayette, and Comte de Rochambeau surrounded the land around the mouth of the Chesapeake Bay, effectively cutting off the British escape by land, the French navy sent a fleet of warships to block Cornwallis, who soon found his troops entirely closed in—with no escape by water.

# ACTIVITIES

## The Battle of Yorktown

Students act out an incident from the famous battle of Yorktown to understand the sequence of events and the contributions of some key figures.

.............................................................................

## A Play's the Thing!

### BACKGROUND

Cornwallis' success in Virginia depended on Sir Henry Clinton, the British commander-in-chief in America. Only Clinton could send British ships and soldiers to Cornwallis. But Clinton had his mind on other matters. He feared that the Americans and their French allies, camped near New York, might try to drive him from his headquarters there.

In the play "Spy at Yorktown," students learn how these events finally played themselves out.

### MATERIALS

"Spy at Yorktown" reproducibles (pages 64–69)

### WHAT TO DO

🔔 Distribute copies of "Spy at Yorktown" and have students review the parts.

🔔 Select ten students to take on the speaking roles listed.

🔔 The rest of the class can take turns reading the Narrator parts out loud or pair up to read the speaking parts chorally.

TIP: If you'd like, invite students to create costumes for their characters. For example, students can create a very simple tricorn hat by stapling three separate strips of construction paper together in a triangle shape that fits the crown of their heads. When the strips are stapled together to create the cap, they can attach cotton batting inside the hat to hang around the sides and bottom. It should take on the appearance of a white powdered wig, popular at that time.

### EXTENSION: Keep Playing!

For the thespians in your classroom, check out *Patriotic & Historical Plays for Young People*, edited by Sylvia E. Kamerman (Plays, 1987). This book contains twenty-five one-act plays and programs (including dramas, comedies, and choral readings), featuring George Washington, Molly Pitcher (Mary Ludwig Hayes), Thomas Paine, Paul Revere, Ben Franklin, Marquis de Lafayette, Haym Salomon, Deborah Gannet, and other heroic figures of the Revolution.

# EXTENSION:
## Th-th-th-that's All, Folks!

When the battle of Yorktown ended, it became clear that the war would soon be over. Even so, it took two more years until the Peace Treaty of 1783 would finally be signed. For the British soldiers, waiting in limbo until they could head home again, things must have felt particularly unusual—after all, they were no longer on British territory. Cornwallis and his men must have sensed the oddity of this situation as they laid down their arms and surrendered at Yorktown. Among the other tunes their marching band played that day was this old English nursery rhyme:

> If buttercups buzz
> after the bee;
> If boats were on land,
> churches on sea;
> If ponies rode men,
> and grass ate the cow;
> If cats should be chased
> into holes by the mouse;
> If mammas sold their babies
> to gypsies for half a crown;
> If summer were spring
> and the other way round
> Then all the world would be upside
> down.

For fun, invite students to add to the list of unlikely occurrences that would also suggest that the world suddenly turned upside down! (Encourage them to include things on their lists that would have been relevant in Revolutionary times!)

# REVOLUTIONARY RESOURCES

In what ways did the war in the South differ from what had been going on up North? What similarities existed? Using resources like these, invite students to compare and contrast similarities and differences between the two.

## FICTION

*The Keeping Room*, by Anna Myers (Puffin Books, 1999). When his father leaves South Carolina to fight in the Revolution, thirteen-year-old Joey Kershaw is left to contend with General Cornwallis—especially after his home is chosen as the General's headquarter.

*Cast Two Shadows: The American Revolution in the South*, by Ann Rinaldi (Harcourt Brace, 1998). Caroline Whitaker is destined to become better acquainted with her grandmother, a slave, during British colonel Rawdon's take-over of their South Carolina home—particularly once they set off together to find Caroline's brother, who was injured in the war.

*George Midgett's War*, by Sally Edwards (Scribner's, 1985). A fictional account of why and how a family on North Carolina's Outer Banks decide to help deliver supplies up to Valley Forge in 1777.

## NONFICTION

*Battlefields Across America: Yorktown*, by Michael Weber (Holt, 1997).

*Birth of the Republic* by Alden R. Carter (Franklin Watts, 1988). Discusses the final campaigns of the American Revolution and the structuring of the new nation.

## ON THE WEB

NARA/Digital Classroom/Teaching With Documents

http://www.archives.gov/digital_classroom/lessons/american_revolution_images/revolution_images.html

History and painting of the Surrender of Cornwallis at Yorktown

# Spy at Yorktown
## by Sue Macy

## CAST

**James Armistead,** an American slave

**Lord Charles Cornwallis,** a British general

**Major General William Phillips,** the British commander in Virginia

**Marquis de Lafayette,** a French soldier fighting with the Americans

**Dr. James McHenry,** Lafayette's aide

**General George Washington,** American commander-in-chief

**Carrie,** an American slave

**Mrs. Donnelly,** an American nurse

**Douglas Wade,** Phillips' aide

**British soldier**

**Narrators**

## ACT 1

**Narrator:** It is July 6, 1781, near Williamsburg, Virginia. Lord Cornwallis and his 7,200 British and German troops have just ambushed the American army under the Marquis de Lafayette. Now, Cornwallis camps for the night before moving on.

**Phillips:** That was a clever bit of strategy, sir, tricking Lafayette into thinking we'd already crossed the river.

**Cornwallis:** Yes, William, they walked right into our trap. It seems that the heroic Frenchman isn't as smart as they say.

**Wade:** He almost met his end this time, sir. Had two horses shot right out from under him, I hear.

**Cornwallis:** And if it weren't for Sir Henry, Lafayette and his army would be out of this war for good. Imagine, Clinton ordering us to withdraw to the coast! And just as we have all of Virginia on its knees!

**Narrator:** A soldier appears at Cornwallis' tent. With him is a black man, barefoot and dressed in worn-out clothing.

**Soldier:** Excuse me, sir, but we found this man at the edge of camp. He says he'd like to speak with you.

**Cornwallis:** Let him speak.

**James:** Thank you, sir. I was telling this soldier that my master's farm was burned down, so I have no place to go. I was wondering if you could use someone to help out around your camp.

**Phillips:** You support the British, do you?

**James:** Yes, sir.

**Phillips:** And why is that?

**James:** Well, sir, this has been your country from the start, and I don't see why that should change.

**Phillips:** True enough.

**Cornwallis:** What's your name, son, and who is your master?

**James:** I'm James, sir. I belong to William Armistead of New Kent County. My master says I can stay with you if you need me.

**Cornwallis:** Sure, James, I think we can use you. First thing in the morning, you can help us break camp. Soldier, take James and get him something to eat.

**Narrator:** They leave.

**Phillips:** He might come in handy.

**Cornwallis:** That's just what I was thinking. I expect the Americans wouldn't take much notice of another black man in their camp. Young James might be just the person to keep us informed of Lafayette's plans.

**Wade:** A spy, sir?

**Cornwallis:** Exactly, Douglas. A spy.

## ACT 2

**Narrator:** The next day, Cornwallis and his army start for Portsmouth, Virginia. The Americans under Lafayette are following close behind. On July 27, Cornwallis sends James to spy on the Americans.

**Mrs. Donnelly:** Hey! You there! Get away from the General's tent. No one is allowed there.

**James:** I've got to see General Lafayette, Ma'am. It's important.

**Mrs. Donnelly:** Important, indeed! The General's had the fever all night, and he's not about to see anyone. If it's so important, you can talk to Dr. McHenry. Here he comes now.

**McHenry:** You look upset, Mrs. Donnelly. It's not the General's condition, I hope.

**Mrs. Donnelly:** No, sir. General Lafayette's been much better this morning. It's this man here. Says he has to see the General.

**McHenry:** You're James Armistead, aren't you?

**James:** Yes, sir.

**McHenry:** And you've got news for the General?

**James:** Yes, sir.

**McHenry:** All right, come with me. Mrs. Donnelly, I'll take care of this.

**Narrator:** They enter Lafayette's tent to find the General sitting on the edge of his cot.

**Lafayette:** I heard all the noises outside, James. I hope my nurse didn't give you a hard time.

**James:** Not really, sir. I'm sorry you're not well.

**Lafayette:** It's nothing that won't pass. Now James, what's the news from the British?

**James:** They'll be moving out sir, as soon as I get back. They've already started loading their ships.

**Lafayette:** They must be going to Baltimore. That's what the rumors have been all along.

**James:** I don't know, sir. I tried to find out where they are headed, but I couldn't. I suppose Lord Cornwallis doesn't really trust me.

**McHenry:** And with good reason, you being our most valuable spy!

**Lafayette:** Cornwallis doesn't know that, thank heavens. At any rate, we've got to get moving. We'll break camp today and head for Baltimore. James, if you get any more information about Cornwallis' plans, try to meet us on the road. We'll be going by way of Richmond.

**James:** Yes, sir, I will. Is there anything you'd like me to tell the British?

**Lafayette:** Yes. Tell them that my men are sick, and that many have deserted. Let Cornwallis think he's got us beaten.

**James:** I will. I hope you feel better, sir.

**Lafayette:** Thank you, James. Good luck to you.

## ACT 3

**Narrator:** James finds out Cornwallis' plans on August 1, when the British troops land at Yorktown, Virginia. He sends a messenger named Carrie to tell Lafayette about this. She returns to Yorktown on August 8, as James is helping to build a dirt wall around the town.

**Carrie:** General Lafayette sends his best, James.

**James:** Hush up, Carrie. Someone might hear you. Now tell me: Did you have any trouble finding the Americans?

**Carrie:** No, they were at Richmond, just as you said. The General was mighty surprised that Cornwallis decided to stay at Yorktown, though. Says His Lordship might have got his British army trapped, with its back to the sea.

**James:** I've been thinking about that. If the French block the York River and the Americans surround the city on land, Cornwallis *will* be trapped.

**Carrie:** That's what Lafayette is trying to arrange. He's already sent a message to General Washington, asking him to come to Virginia with all his troops.

**James:** Washington is up in New Jersey, isn't he?

**Carrie:** Yes. He's been trying to get New York back from the British. But Lafayette says that Yorktown might be more important.

**James:** Yep. It looks like Lord Cornwallis might help put this old tobacco port back on the map.

## ACT 4

**Narrator:** Lafayette and his troops set up camp in Williamsburg, only 14 miles from Yorktown. On August 31, the French fleet creates a blockade off the coast of Yorktown. Now, British ships can't come to Cornwallis' aid. Two weeks later, James sneaks out of the city to bring Lafayette some important news.

**James:** Dr. McHenry! Dr. McHenry!

**McHenry:** James! You must have run all the way from Yorktown. Your news is good, I hope.

**James:** Yes, sir, very good! Where is the General?

**McHenry:** He's across the camp, meeting with General Washington. Washington and his men just arrived from the North. I'll take you to them.

**Narrator:** They find Lafayette reviewing Washington's troops.

67

**Lafayette:** Welcome, James. I'd like you to meet General Washington. And this is Count de Rochambeau, commander of the French troops in America.

**James:** I'm honored, sirs.

**Lafayette:** Gentlemen, James here has been doing some undercover work for us in Yorktown. What's the news, James?

**James:** It's wonderful, General. The French fleet has beaten the British!

**Lafayette:** Hallelujah! Tell us more!

**James:** On September 5, the British fleet under Admiral Graves tried to break the French blockade of Yorktown. But the French pushed them back, and Graves has retreated to New York.

**Washington:** Long live France! What would we Americans do without you?

**Lafayette:** How is Cornwallis taking the setback, James?

**James:** He's hoping Admiral Graves will return, sir.

**Washington:** We've got to move quickly, before Graves does come back.

**Lafayette:** Yes. And James, tell Cornwallis that our army is bigger and healthier than ever. Let him realize that the upper hand is now ours.

# ACT 5

**Narrator:** By September 28, Washington, Lafayette, and Rochambeau have set up camp outside Yorktown. On October 9, their troops start shelling the British base. Six days later, Cornwallis talks with General Phillips.

**Cornwallis:** We can't hold out much longer here. We're running out of food, and the Americans have destroyed most of our buildings with those horrible cannons.

**Phillips:** You've had no news about Admiral Graves?

**Cornwallis:** Sir Henry keeps sending word that the fleet is almost ready to leave New York. But "almost" isn't good enough.

**Phillips:** If only we could stop those American cannons. Then we might be able to overrun the enemy, or at least get supplies in by land.

**Cornwallis:** Yes, we'll have to try. Go and get James Armistead, will you?

**Narrator:** Phillips returns with James.

**Cornwallis:** James, you've been in the enemy's camp. Tell me, where do you think the enemy's line of fire is weakest?

**James:** I'm not sure, sir. Maybe where the French and American sections meet.

**Cornwallis:** I thought so. You may go, James.

**Narrator:** James leaves. But he stays close enough to overhear Cornwallis' conversation.

**Cornwallis:** We'll attack tonight, William. We'll go in where the French and American sections meet. Help me get together 350 of our best men. Our only chance is to silence those guns.

**Narrator:** The British sneak behind enemy lines at 3 a.m., October 16. But the French and Americans are waiting for them. Cornwallis' plan to silence the cannons fails.

**Narrator:** At 10 a.m., on October 17, the British raise a white flag, surrendering. The Americans have won the Battle of Yorktown. It turns out to be the last major battle of the Revolution.

**Narrator:** A few days after the surrender, Lord Cornwallis visits Lafayette's headquarters. There, among the American soldiers, he is shocked to see James Armistead, Lafayette's favorite spy.

**Narrator:** Soon after the Revolution, James Armistead changes his name to James Lafayette. In 1786, the state government of Virginia honors James for his part in the war by making him a free man.

# PART 8

# Epilogue—Freedom Songs

**FOCUS:**

*In what ways did the efforts of African Americans, Native Americans, women, and other marginalized groups during the American Revolution help them win personal freedoms for themselves and their descendants?*

## INTRODUCTION

When the Revolution began, only 2,500,000 people lived in the colonies. Of these, about half a million were of African descent, and most of these were slaves. By the end of the war, about 60,000 slaves had been set free. That's because many had helped to win the nation's freedom, and others because their contributions helped to pass laws which led to the abolishment of slavery in the Northern states.

As the selections in this volume readily show, women and blacks—as well as other groups not represented by the leaders of colonial governments—took on the roles of writers, poets, rebels, spies, and more during the American Revolution. In this section, students have an opportunity to find out how their efforts paid off in the form of improved conditions for their own people.

# ACTIVITIES

# Whose Revolution?

Students read and write to determine the perspectives and choices of marginalized groups during the American Revolution.

## Which Side Are You On?

### BACKGROUND

African Americans, in particular, faced a tricky situation when it came to choosing sides in the American Revolution. In November, 1775, Virginia's royal governor, Lord Dunmore, issued a proclamation. "I hereby…declare all… Negroes…free, that are able and willing to bear arms, they joining his Majesty's troops…," it said.

Of course, with the British tempting blacks to join their side, the colonists soon followed suit. Shortly after Dunmore's announcement, free blacks started joining General Washington's army. Many states also accepted black slaves and freemen among their ranks. (In the case of slaves, the government compensated the slave owners with $1,000 for their "property"; the slaves were offered $50 plus their freedom after the war.)

As African Americans of that time were well aware, choosing either side came with serious risks. First, those who had been slaves had no guarantees that the colonists or the British would honor their agreement. (In truth, they often didn't.) And, of course, these agreements were only worth something if that side won the war. If it turned out they'd thrown their lot in with the losing side, they had no idea how the "enemy" would treat them. Thus, though they were fighting for their freedom, just like the Patriots, they had no idea whether the Patriots

or the redcoats were more likely to give it to them!

### WHAT TO DO

🔔 Considering the options slaves were given to fight for the British or the Patriots during the Revolution, ask students which side—if either—might they have chosen to fight for?

🔔 Working in small groups, have students discuss the question. Then have each team make a T-chart, listing pros and cons for choosing either side, or for remaining neutral in the war.

## Both Sides Now

### BACKGROUND

A historical meeting of Abenaki Indians on a scouting mission for King George and peace-loving Quakers took place in the summer of 1777 near Saratoga, New York. In his book *The Arrow Over the Door*, Joseph Bruchac uses a special literary device: He alternates between the viewpoint of his two main characters— Samuel Russell, a 14-year-old Quaker boy, and Stands Straight, a young Abenaki Indian.

### MATERIALS

*The Arrow Over the Door* by Joseph Bruchac (Dial, 1998)

### WHAT TO DO

🔔 Make sure students discuss the cultural background of the Abenaki and the Quakers and the role each group played in the war. Ask students to think about the types of conflicts that might have arisen between a Quaker and an Abenaki Indian in the British Army during the Revolution.

🔔 Read *The Arrow Over the Door* aloud to the class or have students read it individually.

Then have them think of other people with very opposite viewpoints who might have come into contact with one another during the war (a Tory and a rebel; a mother and her son about to become a solider; a British tax collector and a colonial shop keeper), and create a story or dialogue that highlights their conflicting views.

# A Taste of Their Own Medicine

## BACKGROUND

Paul Cuffe was an anomaly of the Revolutionary era. Despite being the son of a West African-born former-slave father and Wompanoag Indian mother, he became rich! More than that, though, Cuffe was a rebel. In 1775, when the government told him that he owed a lot of money in taxes, he refused to pay, citing the same rationale the colonists used for going to war: taxation without representation! As long as he and other African Americans were denied the right to vote, he said, he would not pay!

Thanks to Cuffe's efforts, Massachusetts granted free black adult males the right to vote in 1783.

## MATERIALS

**What Liberty Means to Me reproducible (page 13)**

## WHAT TO DO

🔔 If students have completed the poem from page 13, have them find and review their original poem. Otherwise, distribute copies of the What Liberty Means to Me reproducible now.

🔔 Keeping Cuffe's situation in mind, invite students to rewrite this poem or write a new poem from Cuffe's point of view.

🔔 If students rewrite their original poem, ask

whether the same feelings about freedom apply in their new version? If so, why? If not, how would their poems have to change?

## DID YOU KNOW...?

In 1781, a Massachusetts slave named Mum Bett sued for and won her freedom under the state constitution! In fact, most slaves of that era who entered these types of lawsuits, won. However, very few ever took their cases to court. For one thing, not all African Americans knew of the law. And of those who did, many could not afford the expense of a trial. Others were probably too afraid to challenge their masters to even consider taking the risk.

## REVOLUTIONARY RESOURCES

*The Bloody Country*, by James Lincoln Collier and Christopher Collier (Scholastic, 1976). Ben Buck learns what freedom really means when his best friend, his father's half-black, half-Native American slave, is freed.

*Venture for Freedom: The True Story of an African Yankee*, by Ruby Zagoren (World, 1969). Based on the autobiography of the son of a West African tribal king, Venture Smith, who was captured by slave traders at age 7 and brought to America.

*Braving the New World, 1619-1784: Milestones in Black American History*, by Don Nardo (Chelsea House, 1994). Covers the period from the arrival of the first enslaved Africans to the end of the American Revolution.

*Black Heroes of the American Revolution*, by Burke Davis (Harcourt Brace Jovanovich, 1976).

*Revolutionary Citizens: African Americans 1776-1804*, by Daniel C. Littlefield (Oxford University Press, 1997). A history of African Americans from the fifteenth through the twentieth century.

*Come All You Brave Soldiers*, by Clinton Cox (Scholastic, 1999). About the black soldiers who fought for America in the war.